Let's make money
Adrian Reyes

Copyright © 2024 by Adrian Reyes

All rights reserved.

No portion of this book may be reproduced in any form without written permission from the publisher or author, except as permitted by U.S. copyright law.

Contents

Chapter	1
Introduction	2
Chapter 1 **The Role of Motivation in Personal Finance**	13
Chapter 2 **Developing a Growth Mindset for Financial Success**	51
Chapter 3 **Building Wealth Through Habits**	68
Chapter 4 **Overcoming Financial Setbacks and Staying Motivated**	101

Chapter 5   129
Shifting Your Mindset from Spending to Investing

Chapter 6   153
Financial Freedom and the Final Push

Chapter 7   169
The power of savings

*To the ones who couldn't make it to the end
of the month, but are still trying.*

Introduction

You've heard it before: "Money can't buy happiness." And sure, it's true in a Hallmark-card sense. But let's face it, money makes life a whole lot easier. It lets you breathe easier when the bills are due, indulge in the occasional splurge, and avoid having to decide between guacamole and a full tank of gas. For most of us, financial peace isn't about private jets or sprawling mansions. It's about not waking up in a cold sweat, wondering if this month's paycheck will cover next month's rent.

The truth is, you don't need to be rich to live richly. You just need to think differently about money. That's what this book is about; teaching you how to make smarter choices, shift your mindset, and live large even if your bank account isn't bragging six-figure numbers.

Imagine this: You wake up on a sunny Saturday morning, grab your favorite cup of coffee, and take a walk without a single worry about how you're going to pay for groceries, utilities, or the occasional brunch. You're not chasing million-dollar dreams or glued to a hustle culture that promises wealth but leaves you burned out. You're simply living your life comfortably, confidently, and on your terms.

Sounds good, right? The best part is, it's achievable.

Why This Book?

Here's the thing: The financial world loves to overcomplicate things. You'll hear about portfolios, diversification, market volatility, and other intimidating jargon. Or you'll be told the only way to "make it" is by building a tech empire, flipping real estate, or becoming an influencer. But let's be honest, that's not for everyone. And it doesn't have to be.

This book is different. It's not a get-rich-quick guide, nor is it a dry textbook on personal finance. It's a practical, no-BS approach to mastering your money. It's about creating a life where your finances work for you, not the other way around. Whether you're drowning in debt, living paycheck-to-paycheck, or simply looking for ways to maximize your income, this book will meet you where you are and guide you forward.

We're going to talk about how to:

Shift your mindset to stop feeling broke, even if you aren't rich.

Master simple financial strategies that build wealth over time, without the burnout.

Maximize every dollar, so your money works smarter, not harder.

Avoid lifestyle inflation and find joy in what truly matters.

Create a financial plan that aligns with your goals, values, and happiness.

This isn't about deprivation or cutting out every little indulgence. You can have your avocado toast and eat it too. It's about making intentional choices so you can enjoy the present while building a secure future. And yes, it's entirely possible to live well without breaking the bank.

The Power of Mindset

Before we dive into the nitty-gritty of budgets, saving strategies, and financial goals, let's talk about the one thing that can make or break your financial success: your mindset.

Money isn't just numbers in a bank account; it's deeply tied to our emotions, habits, and beliefs. Many of us grow up with limiting money stories:

"I'll never make enough to feel secure."

"Rich people are greedy or selfish."

"If I'm not making six figures, I'll always struggle."

Sound familiar? These stories are more common than you think. But here's the good news: They're just stories. And stories can be rewritten.

In this book, we'll explore how to cultivate a mindset that empowers you to take control of your money without fear, guilt, or shame. You'll learn to see money as a tool, not a source of stress. It's not about how much you earn; it's about how you manage, grow, and prioritize what you have.

Why Financial freedom isn't just for the wealthy

Let's address the elephant in the room: The world loves to glamorize wealth. From reality TV stars flashing their designer wardrobes to billionaires launching rockets into space, the message is clear: financial freedom is reserved for the ultra-rich. But that's a lie.

Financial freedom isn't about yachts or private islands; it's about choices. It's the ability to say yes to what matters and no to what doesn't. It's the freedom to pursue your passions, spend time with loved ones, and live without constant financial stress. And you don't need to be rich to achieve it.

Consider this: A teacher earning $50,000 a year with no debt and a clear financial plan can have more freedom than a lawyer earning $200,000 but drowning in credit card bills and a mortgage they can barely afford. It's not about the number in your bank account; it's about what that number allows you to do.

In the pages ahead, we'll explore how to create a financial life that gives you peace, security, and the freedom to enjoy what truly matters. No lottery wins, no trust funds, just smart, intentional choices.

Living large on a small budget

Here's the real secret: You don't need a six-figure salary to live a rich, fulfilling life. You just need to master the balance between spending wisely and enjoying the things that make you happy.

Living large on a small budget doesn't mean deprivation. It means prioritizing. It means saying yes to experiences that bring you joy and no to the things that don't. It means getting creative with your spending, finding ways to indulge without going into debt, and learning to appreciate the value of what you already have.

For example:

Travel doesn't have to mean luxury resorts; it can mean budget-friendly road trips, off-season adventures, or using credit card points wisely.

Dining out doesn't have to be a splurge; it can mean finding hidden gems, cooking with friends, or enjoying the occasional treat without guilt.

Entertainment doesn't have to break the bank but it can mean taking advantage of free events, exploring nature, or rediscovering hobbies you love.

In this book, I'll share practical strategies for stretching your dollars without feeling stretched thin. You'll learn how to create a budget that works for your lifestyle, avoid the trap of lifestyle inflation, and build a life that feels rich, no matter what your income is.

What this book will teach you

This isn't a one-size-fits-all approach to money. Everyone's financial journey is different, and this book is designed to help you find what works for you. Here's a preview of what you'll learn:

The Foundation of Financial Freedom: How to shift your mindset, set clear goals, and build habits that support your financial success.

Mastering Money Management: Simple strategies for budgeting, saving, and paying off debt without sacrificing your happiness.

Living Well Today and Tomorrow: How to balance enjoying life now with planning for the future.

Building Wealth Your Way: Smart, sustainable ways to grow your wealth over time, even if you're starting small.

Staying Motivated: Tips for overcoming setbacks, staying on track, and celebrating your progress.

This isn't about perfection. You don't need to have it all figured out, and you don't need to become a financial expert overnight. This is about taking small, intentional steps toward a life where money is a source of empowerment, not stress.

By the end of this book, you'll have the tools, mindset, and confidence to take control of your financial future. You'll learn to live richly without debt, without stress, and without sacrificing what matters most. So, buckle up. You're about to transform your relationship with money and, in the process, transform your life.

"Let's get started, because financial freedom isn't about being rich; it's about being smart, intentional, and free to enjoy the life you truly want."

Your journey begins now.

Chapter 1
THE ROLE OF MOTIVATION IN PERSONAL FINANCE

Let's understand here the link between Motivation and Financial Success.

Motivation is the engine behind financial decisions. Whether it's the desire to save for the future, invest wisely, or pay off debt, motivation drives action. But motivation is more than just a feeling; it's an ongoing force that needs to be cultivated and maintained.

I want to talk about a subject that is central to so many of our lives: motivation to achieve financial goals. Whether you're saving for a dream home, planning for retirement, or striving to start your own business, motivation plays a crucial role in turning financial aspirations into reality.

Financial goals are more than aspirations, they are the bedrock of financial stability and independence. They give our money purpose, guiding our choices and helping us prioritize what truly matters. They provide direction, turning aimless spending into intentional action and short-term sacrifices into meaningful progress. Yet, setting a financial goal is only the first step. The true challenge lies in maintaining the motivation to see it through, especially in the face of life's inevitable obstacles such as unexpected expenses, shifting priorities, or the allure of instant gratification.

Motivation is not just a fleeting burst of energy; it is the steady engine that drives us forward. It transforms a vague dream into a tangible plan and sustains us when the path grows difficult. Without motivation, even the most carefully crafted financial plan can falter. Let's explore how motivation plays a critical role in achieving financial goals:

Financial success is rarely immediate; it's a marathon, not a sprint. Motivation helps us keep our eyes on the prize, providing the clarity to remember why we began the journey. Whether it's the dream of home ownership, the freedom of a debt-free life, or the promise of early retirement, visualization is a powerful tool. Picture the moment you achieve your goal: the keys to your first home in your hand, the warmth of a sunset in your dream destination, or the peaceful realization that your financial future is secure. This vivid image transforms an abstract idea into an emotional anchor, making the sacrifices along the way, skipping a luxury purchase or sticking to a strict budget, feel meaningful and worthwhile.

Financial planning is not a straight path; it's a road paved with unexpected detours. Emergencies arise, investments may underperform, and moments of doubt can test your resolve. Motivation is the inner strength that helps you weather these storms. It reminds you that progress is not linear, and every small victory brings you closer to your ultimate goal. Celebrating milestones along the way, whether it's paying off a small debt, reaching a savings benchmark, or successfully sticking to your budget for a month, reignites your determination. These moments of progress, no matter how modest, reaffirm that you are on the right track.

While motivation is the spark that ignites the fire, discipline and habits are the fuel that keeps it burning. Motivation helps establish the foundation for consistent financial behaviors; creating a budget, setting aside savings, or regularly contributing to investments. Over time, these actions become second nature, requiring less effort to maintain. Even when motivation wanes, as it inevitably does, the habits you've built will carry you forward. This synergy between motivation and discipline creates a cycle of success: motivation inspires action, action builds momentum, and momentum sustains motivation.

Motivation is the catalyst that transforms financial aspirations into reality. It keeps us focused on the long-term vision, fortifies us against challenges, and helps us build the habits necessary for sustained success. Achieving financial goals is not merely about numbers on a spreadsheet; it's about aligning our actions with our deepest values and aspirations. By cultivating and nurturing motivation, we ensure that our journey toward financial stability and independence is not only achievable but deeply rewarding.

Here are some practical strategies to maintain your motivation:

*Set **SMART** Financial Goals*

Make them Specific, Measurable, Achievable, Relevant, and Time-bound. For example, instead of saying, "I want to save money," set a goal like, "I will save $10,000 in two years for a down payment on a house."

Break it down

Dividing your goal into smaller, manageable milestones is a proven strategy rooted in psychological and practical principles. Large, ambitious goals can often feel overwhelming or distant, making it difficult to stay motivated. Breaking them down into achievable steps transforms what might seem insurmountable into a series of attainable actions, providing clarity and a sense of direction.

Why milestones matter?

- Clarity and focus:
  Smaller milestones help to simplify the complexity of a larger goal. Instead of being daunted by the entirety of the task, milestones allow you to concentrate on specific actions or phases. For example, instead of focusing on "saving $10,000," you might aim to save $500 a month. This focused approach provides a clear roadmap, reducing anxiety and boosting confidence.

- Psychological wins:
  Achieving a milestone, no matter how small, triggers a sense of accomplishment. This is tied to the brain's reward system, where the release of dopamine reinforces positive behavior. These "mini-victories" serve as motivational boosts, reminding you that

progress is being made and inspiring you to tackle the next step with renewed energy.

- Building momentum:
Success breeds success. Each milestone you achieve builds momentum, making the next step feel more within reach. Momentum is a powerful motivator and it transforms small actions into a compounding force that propels you forward.

- Reinforcing self-belief:
Every milestone met reinforces the belief that the larger goal is achievable. This gradual build-up of confidence counteracts doubt and discouragement. Over time, this belief becomes a self-fulfilling prophecy: the more you accomplish, the more capable you feel of completing the entire journey.

Celebrating mini-victories

Celebrating milestones is not just about indulgence; it's about reinforcing the progress you've made and giving yourself permission to acknowledge your efforts. Here's why this matters:

- Sustained motivation: Recognizing achievements, no matter how minor, creates positive associations with the process. This keeps you engaged and motivated to continue working toward the next milestone.

- Emotional balance: The path to a significant goal can be draining, both emotionally and physically. Celebrations provide moments of joy and relief, helping to combat burnout and maintain a positive outlook.

- Reframing sacrifice: Celebrations remind you that the journey isn't just about the destination. They transform the sacrifices, like cutting back on unnecessary spending or working extra hours, into stepping stones toward success.

How to implement milestones effectively?

- Define specific steps: Break your goal into actionable, measurable chunks. For instance, if your goal is to pay off $15,000 in debt, divide it into $1,000 increments with specific timelines.

- Track your progress: Use a visual tracker or journal to monitor each milestone. Seeing your progress in tangible form enhances motivation.

- Plan celebrations: Align your rewards

with your journey. After saving a set amount, treat yourself to something modest but meaningful, like a favorite meal or a small gift.

Track your progress

Tracking progress is a cornerstone of achieving any goal, particularly financial ones, because it provides tangible evidence of your efforts and outcomes. The process of monitoring not only keeps you informed but also serves as a psychological motivator, reinforcing positive behaviors and allowing you to adjust your strategies as needed. Whether through budgeting apps, spreadsheets, or even a notebook, the act of tracking creates a framework for accountability and success.

Why tracking progress is essential?

- Visibility and awareness:
Financial goals often involve numerous moving parts, income, expenses, savings, and investments. Without tracking, it's easy to lose sight of these details and miss opportunities for improvement. A clear record of your financial activities highlights where your money is going and how it aligns with your goals.

- Motivation through measurable progress:
Seeing concrete evidence of your progress is incredibly motivating. For instance, watching your savings account grow or your debt balance shrink reminds you that your efforts are paying off. These visual cues reaffirm your commitment and make the abstract goal feel achievable.

- Accountability:
  Tracking introduces a level of accountability by creating a record of your decisions. This accountability discourages impulsive actions, like unnecessary splurges, because the consequences are immediately visible in your tracking tool.

- Adaptability and control:
  Financial journeys are rarely linear. Unexpected expenses or changes in income can disrupt your plans. By tracking regularly, you can identify these disruptions early and adjust your strategy to stay on course. For example, if an expense reduces your ability to save one month, you can plan to compensate in the following months.

The benefits of using tools

- Budgeting apps:
  Apps like Mint, YNAB (You Need A Budget), or PocketGuard are tailored for financial tracking. They automatically categorize expenses, provide real-time updates, and generate visual reports that make understanding your financial landscape easy and intuitive.

- Spreadsheets:
  A simple spreadsheet offers flexibility and customization. With tools like Excel or Google Sheets, you can create personalized trackers tailored to your specific goals, from savings targets to debt repayment schedules. Spreadsheets are particularly useful for those who enjoy hands-on control over their data.

- Physical tracking:
  For some, manually noting progress in a journal or planner is a tactile and re-

warding experience. This method can be combined with visual aids like charts or progress bars to make milestones feel even more tangible.

How tracking enhances motivation?

- Celebrating milestones: As you record each small victory, like hitting a savings benchmark or paying off a credit card, you experience a psychological boost that keeps you motivated.

- Turning data into action: Regular reviews of your tracked data allow you to identify patterns, such as overspending in certain categories, and take corrective action before it becomes a larger issue.

- Building confidence: Consistent tracking provides undeniable proof of your ability to make progress. This builds confidence in your capacity to achieve your larger financial goals.

Best practices for tracking progress

- Set regular Check-ins: Review your tracking tool weekly or monthly to stay updated on your progress and make adjustments.

- Be honest and thorough: Record all expenses and income accurately to get a true picture of your financial health.

- Use visuals: Graphs, charts, or color-coded trackers make your progress more engaging and easier to understand.

Visualize success

Visualization is a powerful psychological technique that turns abstract goals into vivid, tangible aspirations. By creating a clear mental picture of what success looks like, you connect emotionally with your goals, making them feel more real and attainable. Visual tools like a vision board or a photo of your desired outcome reinforce this connection, serving as daily reminders of why you're striving and helping you stay focused amidst distractions.

Why visualization works?

- Harnessing emotional connection: Goals that are purely logical or numerical can sometimes feel detached and impersonal. Visualization bridges this gap by tying your aspirations to emotions. For instance, seeing a photo of your dream home isn't just a reminder of your financial goal; it evokes feelings of comfort, pride, and accomplishment.

These emotions provide a strong motivator to keep working toward your target.

- Engaging the subconscious mind:
Visualization taps into your subconscious, programming your mind to focus on the actions needed to achieve your goal. This process aligns your thoughts, decisions, and behaviors with your desired outcome. By regularly seeing visual cues of success, you subconsciously prioritize tasks and habits that bring you closer to your objective.

- Reinforcing motivation:
A clear image of your goal makes sacrifices feel worthwhile. For example, skipping a luxury purchase becomes easier when you can see how that saved money contributes to something meaningful, like a family vacation or paying off

debt. Visual reminders anchor you to your "why," keeping you inspired during challenging moments.

- Boosting positivity and resilience: Visualization creates a positive mindset. Instead of focusing on obstacles or setbacks, you're consistently reminded of what's possible. This focus on the positive builds resilience, encouraging you to persevere even when progress seems slow.

Using visual tools effectively

1. Vision boards:

    ○ What they are: A vision board is a collage of images, words, and symbols that represent your goals. For financial aspirations, this might include pictures of a dream car, home, or travel destination, along with motivational quotes or numbers that signify your savings targets.

- How it helps: The process of creating a vision board forces you to clarify your goals, breaking them down into specific, visual elements. Displaying it in a prominent place keeps those goals front and center in your daily life.

2. Photos or symbols:

- What they are: A single photo or object that embodies your goal, for example, a picture of a college campus you're saving for or a passport to represent your travel dreams.

- How it helps: Simple, focused reminders are easy to integrate into your daily routine. Placing them on your desk, fridge, or phone lock screen ensures frequent exposure.

3. Daily visualization practices:

- What it is: Spending a few moments each day imagining yourself achieving your goal, walking into your new home, seeing a zero balance on a debt statement, or experiencing the joy of a dream vacation.

- How it helps: Repetition strengthens your belief in your ability to succeed and fosters a sense of anticipation and excitement about the journey ahead.

The science behind visualization

Research in neuroscience suggests that the brain doesn't distinguish much between vividly imagining an experience and actually living it. This means that visualizing success can trigger similar neural pathways as real achievement, priming your brain for the actions required to turn the vision into reality. Studies have shown that visualization increases confidence, improves focus, and enhances goal-directed behavior.

Best practices for visualization

- Make it specific: Vague goals like "be financially stable" are harder to visualize. Instead, focus on concrete outcomes, such as "save $20,000 for a down payment" or "pay off $5,000 in debt within two years."

- Revisit regularly: Consistency is key. Make visualization a daily habit, whether by looking at your vision board or spending five minutes imagining success.

- Combine with action: Visualization is a

tool, not a replacement for effort. Use it to stay motivated, but back it up with actionable steps.

Surround yourself with support

The journey to achieving any goal, especially financial ones, is rarely a solo endeavor. Surrounding yourself with a supportive network—friends, family, mentors, or even like-minded peers—can significantly enhance your chances of success. Support systems provide encouragement, accountability, and perspective, acting as a safety net when challenges arise and a cheering section when you make progress. Sharing your goals with others is not just about seeking validation; it's about creating an environment that fosters motivation, accountability, and growth.

Why support matters?

- Encouragement during challenges:
  The path to financial success is filled with obstacles, from unexpected expenses to moments of doubt. A supportive network offers encouragement when motivation wanes. Hearing a friend say, "You've got this," or a mentor remind you of your progress can be the push you need to stay focused during tough times.

- Accountability:
  Sharing your goals with others creates a sense of responsibility. When you tell someone about your plans, like saving for a down payment or paying off debt, you're more likely to stick to them. Accountability partners can check in on your progress, celebrate your victories, and gently remind you of your commitments if you falter.

- Perspective and guidance:
  Trusted mentors or financially experienced friends can provide invaluable insights and advice. They can help you avoid common pitfalls, offer strategies for overcoming obstacles, and share lessons from their own journeys. Sometimes, an outside perspective is all it takes to clarify your next steps.

- Reinforcement of positive habits:
  Being surrounded by individuals who share similar goals or values can reinforce your own commitment. For example, spending time with friends who prioritize saving or avoiding unnecessary spending can inspire you to maintain those habits as well. Positive peer influence becomes a motivator rather than a distraction.

The psychological benefits of support

Research shows that social support enhances emotional well-being and resilience, which are critical when pursuing long-term goals. Sharing your ambitions with others reduces feelings of isolation, provides a sense of belonging, and creates a built-in support system for celebrating progress or navigating setbacks.

How to build and leverage support systems?

- Share strategically:
  Be intentional about who you share your goals with. Choose people who are trustworthy, supportive, and aligned with your values. This could include close friends, family members, colleagues, or even a financial advisor.

- Create an accountability partner system:
  Partner with someone who has a similar

goal or mindset. For example, if you're saving for a big purchase, find someone who is also working toward financial independence. Schedule regular check-ins to discuss progress, challenges, and next steps.

- Seek mentorship:
  A mentor with experience in financial planning or goal-setting can provide tailored advice and encouragement. Their perspective can help you navigate challenges more effectively and stay motivated.

- Engage in communities:
  Join online forums, social media groups, or local meetups dedicated to financial topics. Engaging with a community of like-minded individuals creates a sense of camaraderie and provides access to shared resources and strategies.

- Celebrate together:
  Share your milestones with your support system, whether it's paying off a credit card, hitting a savings goal, or sticking to your budget for six months. Celebrating with others reinforces the positive behaviors that helped you succeed.

Balancing independence with support

While support is invaluable, it's essential to maintain ownership of your goals. Your support system is there to assist, not to dictate or control your journey. Use their encouragement and advice as tools to enhance your progress while staying true to your own vision and values.

Reward yourself along the way

Plan small rewards for achieving milestones. Treating yourself in moderation can prevent burnout and keep the journey enjoyable.

Remember, motivation gets you started, but consistency is what leads to success. As the saying goes, "A journey of a thousand miles begins with a single step." In the context of financial goals, that step might be creating a budget, setting up an emergency fund, or making your first investment. Each step brings you closer to your goal.

In closing, I want to remind you that achieving financial goals is not just about money, it's about the freedom, security, and opportunities that financial success brings. Motivation is the fuel that powers this journey, but the real reward lies in what those financial goals allow you to do: provide for your loved ones, pursue your passions, and live life on your terms.

So, stay motivated, stay disciplined, and remember: every small decision you make today is a step toward a brighter financial future. Let's commit to taking those steps together, one day at a time.

The Dreamer and the Doubter

In a small town nestled between rolling hills, there lived two childhood friends, Emma and Jack. Both grew up in modest households, where their parents worked hard to make ends meet. However, the two friends took very different approaches to money as they entered adulthood.

Emma was always the dreamer. From an early age, she envisioned herself becoming financially independent. She dreamed of owning a house by the lake, traveling the world, and running her own business. But Emma didn't just dream; she acted. She studied personal finance, listened to podcasts, read books, and took every opportunity to learn about investing, saving, and building wealth. Most importantly, she kept herself motivated by focusing on her long-term goals.

Jack, on the other hand, was more cautious and sceptical. He often thought that financial independence was only for the lucky few or those with a higher income. "It's easier for people who have a head start," Jack would say. "Money just doesn't work like it's supposed to for people like me." Jack believed that working hard at his job would eventually pay off, but he never truly understood the importance of motivation or proactive financial planning. He was content to live pay check to pay check, spending a little too freely, and never really saving or investing.

One summer evening, Emma invited Jack to dinner at her apartment. She had recently received an unexpected bonus from her freelance work and had just finished making a large investment in a rental property. The apartment was cozy, yet Emma had transformed it into a space that felt full of promise, like she was preparing for something bigger.

"Jack, you wouldn't believe how far I've come," Emma said, pouring them both a glass of wine. "I've been working on my financial goals for the last few years, and it's paying off. I'm not where I want to be yet, but I'm getting there."

Jack looked at her, somewhat confused. "How are you doing it, Em? You don't make a ton of money. I thought you just took on side gigs for extra cash. Isn't it hard to keep up with all this investing stuff?"

Emma smiled and set her glass down. "It's not about making a ton of money, Jack. It's about being intentional with what I do with the money I do have. It's all about staying motivated, even when it gets tough."

Jack raised an eyebrow. "What do you mean? You always seem so... focused. How do you keep yourself going when you don't see immediate results?"

Emma took a deep breath, thinking for a moment. "Honestly, it starts with motivation. Motivation is the link between what you want and what you're willing to do to get there. I don't just want to be wealthy for the sake of it. I want to live freely, without financial worry. I'm willing to make sacrifices now and cut back on luxuries, invest my time and money wisely, so that I can build something sustainable for the future."

Jack sat back, still processing her words. "But I've always heard it's just about having the right opportunities or connections. It's easy for people who get lucky."

Emma shook her head. "It's not about luck, Jack. Motivation and discipline are the key. It's a mindset shift. I had to change the way I thought about money. Once I did that, everything else followed."

Jack's Revelation.

Over the following weeks, Jack couldn't stop thinking about Emma's words. He noticed that he kept making the same excuses. Every time he thought about setting a budget or saving for the future, he convinced himself that it wasn't worth it because he didn't make enough money or didn't have the right connections. But Emma's passion and determination kept coming back to him.

One day, while having lunch at a café, Jack had a realization. Maybe it wasn't about having everything handed to him. Maybe it was about having the right mindset. He decided to give Emma's approach a try.

Jack started by setting small, realistic financial goals. He began tracking his spending and cutting back on unnecessary purchases. He focused on saving 10% of his income each month, even if it was just a small amount. More importantly, he started learning about investing. He signed up for an online course on personal finance and read about the importance of compound interest and the power of consistent saving.

It wasn't easy at first. Jack struggled with temptation, especially when he wanted to buy new gadgets or eat out at expensive restaurants. But he kept reminding himself of his long-term goals, and slowly, he started seeing progress. Every time he saved a little more or made a smart financial decision, he felt a rush of accomplishment.

The Ripple Effect.

Months went by, and Jack's mindset began to shift. The more he focused on his financial goals, the more motivated he became. He started to see the connection between his actions and his results. He was no longer simply reacting to life's challenges; he was proactively shaping his financial future.

One evening, after attending a networking event, Jack called Emma to share some exciting news. "You won't believe it, Em," he said. "I've started investing in stocks, and I just reached my savings goal for the year. It feels amazing to see my money working for me."

Emma's voice lit up with excitement. "That's incredible, Jack! I'm so proud of you! See? You just needed the right motivation, and now you're on the path to financial freedom."

Jack smiled. "I get it now. It's not about being lucky or waiting for the right opportunity. It's about having the discipline to make the right choices and staying motivated to achieve the things that matter most to me."

Years later, Jack found himself in a place he had once thought was impossible. He had built up a diverse portfolio of investments, had saved up a down payment for a house, and was living a life that was comfortable and secure. He had also transitioned into a new career, one that aligned with his passions and gave him more control over his time.

One afternoon, while sitting on the porch of his new home, Jack reflected on his journey. He thought about his early years and how he had been sceptical and unsure about his ability to achieve financial success. But he also thought about Emma, whose belief in herself and her ability to control her financial future had inspired him to take action. It wasn't about luck; it was about taking charge of his financial destiny and staying motivated, even when it felt like the road ahead was long.

Looking out at the horizon, Jack smiled. He had learned the most important lesson of all: Motivation wasn't just the fuel for his financial success and it had been the catalyst that turned his dreams into reality.

Moral of the Story.

Financial success is neither accidental nor reserved for an elite few. It is the product of motivation, discipline, and a mindset that embraces challenges as opportunities. Like Jack, anyone can achieve financial freedom by understanding the link between motivation and the actions required to reach their goals. It all starts with one intentional choice, followed by another, until success becomes inevitable.

Chapter 2
Developing a Growth Mindset for Financial Success

The *Power of Belief* and how money mindsets shape financial futures.

Imagine your mind as a garden, and your beliefs about money are the seeds you plant. Whether you believe wealth is just for the lucky few, or that you can grow your financial freedom with the right mindset and actions, these beliefs shape how you interact with money every day. Your money mindset influences how you save, spend, invest, and even how you feel about success and failure.

In The Power of Belief, we explore how your thoughts about money can either be a barrier or a springboard to financial prosperity. Whether you're embracing a mindset of abundance, or wrestling with limiting beliefs, your financial future is deeply intertwined with the stories you tell yourself about money. Let's dive into how shifting those beliefs can unlock new possibilities for wealth and well-being!

Whether you're working to pay off debt, build wealth, or achieve financial independence, cultivating a growth mindset can be the game-changer you need to unlock your potential.

A growth mindset, a concept popularized by psychologist Dr. Carol Dweck, is the belief that abilities and intelligence can be developed through effort, learning, and persistence. In contrast to a fixed mindset, where people see their capabilities as static, a growth mindset embraces challenges and views failures as opportunities to grow.

When applied to finances, a growth mindset means believing that you can improve your financial situation, no matter where you're starting from. It's about shifting from "I'll never be good with money" to "I can learn to manage my money better."

Why does a Growth Mindset matter for Financial Success?

A growth mindset is the belief that abilities and intelligence can be developed through dedication, learning, and effort. When applied to financial success, this perspective fosters resilience, adaptability, and a sense of empowerment, qualities essential for navigating the complexities of money management. Many people unintentionally limit their potential by clinging to fixed mindsets, believing they're inherently bad with money or that their circumstances are unchangeable. A growth mindset challenges these beliefs, reframing them as opportunities for improvement and progress.

Financial setbacks are inevitable, whether they take the form of unexpected expenses, job losses, or investment mistakes. These challenges can feel discouraging, but a growth mindset views them as opportunities to learn, adapt, and come back stronger.

- Resilience through perspective:
  A fixed mindset might interpret a financial setback as evidence of failure, leading to frustration or giving up. In contrast, a growth mindset sees setbacks as temporary and solvable. For example, a failed investment becomes a chance to study market trends and refine future

strategies.

- Problem-solving mindset:
  With a growth-oriented approach, financial challenges are reframed as puzzles to solve rather than insurmountable obstacles. This mindset encourages creative solutions, like finding new income streams after a job loss or reworking a budget to accommodate unexpected costs.

Psychological research shows that individuals with a growth mindset are more likely to embrace challenges, persist through difficulties, and see effort as a path to mastery. These traits are critical for financial success, where setbacks are common and adaptability is key.

Neuroplasticity, the brain's ability to adapt and form new connections, supports the idea that financial habits and knowledge can be developed. A growth mindset taps into this potential, fostering a belief in your ability to improve your financial situation over time.

How to Develop a Growth Mindset for Financial Success?

Educate yourself about personal finance through books, podcasts, or online courses. The more you learn, the more empowered you'll feel to make informed decisions.

Adopt the mantra: *"I may not know this yet, but I can learn."*

A clear vision of what you want to achieve financially gives you a sense of direction.

Break big goals into smaller, achievable steps. Each success builds confidence and reinforces your belief in your ability to grow.

Instead of viewing financial mistakes as failures, ask yourself: What can I learn from this?

For example, if an investment didn't yield the expected returns, analyse what went wrong and how you can make better decisions next time.

Focus on what you have achieved so far, no matter how small. Gratitude can shift your mindset from scarcity to abundance, fuelling your motivation to grow further.

Believe that your financial future holds opportunities you can seize with effort and persistence.

Join communities, find mentors, or connect with friends who inspire you to grow financially. Their energy and insights can reinforce your own growth mindset.

Progress comes from action. Start with small changes, like tracking expenses or automating savings, and build on those habits over time.

Remember, the key to growth is consistency, not perfection.

Examples of a Mindset in Action:

Fixed Mindset: *"I'll never earn more money in my career."*

Growth Mindset: *"I can learn new skills to increase my earning potential."*

Fixed Mindset: *"Investing is too complicated for me."*

Growth Mindset: *"I can start by learning the basics and grow my knowledge step by step."*

Fixed Mindset: *"I'm bad at budgeting."*

Growth Mindset: *"I can find a system that works for me and practice until I get better."*

Developing a growth mindset doesn't just lead to financial success, it fosters resilience, confidence, and a sense of control over your life. It helps you build the habits and skills necessary for financial independence, creating opportunities for you to live the life you desire.

As we strive for financial success, remember that your mindset is your most powerful asset. Developing a growth mindset isn't about being perfect or achieving overnight success. It's about believing in your ability to grow, taking consistent action, and turning every challenge into a stepping stone.

So, let's commit to embracing a growth mindset. Let's challenge ourselves to learn, adapt, and persevere. Because with the right mindset, there's no limit to what we can achieve financially and beyond.

The Two Sisters

In a bustling city, there were two sisters, Lily and Sophie, who grew up in the same household, surrounded by the same financial circumstances. Their parents were hard-working, but their income was modest, and they lived a life of simplicity, with little room for luxuries. Yet, despite having similar upbringings, the two sisters had very different beliefs about money and those beliefs would shape the course of their lives in dramatically different ways.

Lily, the older of the two, always had a sense of scarcity around money. She believed that there was never enough to go around. Her parents often spoke of bills piling up and the stress of making ends meet, and Lily internalized these worries as she grew older. She was convinced that financial security was reserved for the fortunate, and that no matter how hard she worked, there would always be a limit to what she could achieve. She took this belief into adulthood and into her career, never feeling truly secure, always worried that a single setback could send her back to square one.

Sophie, on the other hand, had a different perspective. While she witnessed her parents' struggles as well, she chose to believe that money was a tool that could be managed, grown, and leveraged. Sophie was curious about personal finance, and instead of seeing money as something scarce, she saw it as something that could flow freely with the right mindset and strategy. While her sister held tight to the belief that money was difficult to come by, Sophie believed that with the right knowledge and discipline, financial abundance was within reach.

The Diverging paths.

As they grew older, their beliefs about money began to play out in their lives.

Lily went to college, choosing a stable career in accounting. She worked diligently and earned a good salary, but she always felt that no matter how much she earned, it wasn't enough. She was always worried about running out of money, even when there was no immediate reason to worry. She saved cautiously, but also hesitated to invest or take financial risks. Each month, she would check her bank account with a sense of dread, as if expecting the worst. She lived within strict boundaries, refusing to indulge in even modest pleasures, always thinking that one misstep would ruin her future.

On the other hand, Sophie went down a different route. After graduating, she took a job in digital marketing, where the potential for growth was high. Sophie didn't earn as much as Lily, but she approached money with an entirely different mindset. Sophie believed that money wasn't just about earning more—it was about making smart choices and creating opportunities for growth. She invested early in a diversified portfolio, and when she wanted to make a big purchase, like buying a new car or taking a vacation, she didn't rely on credit cards or loans. She saved for it first. Sophie also worked on her skills, learning about investing, entrepreneurship, and passive income streams, believing that her financial situation could improve through knowledge and action.

Over the next decade, their financial situations began to reflect their beliefs.

Lily, despite her stable job, was often anxious about money. She kept her expenses low, but she also avoided investments or exploring side income opportunities. She felt trapped in a cycle where no matter how much she saved, it wasn't enough. Her belief in scarcity led to a lack of financial growth. Even with a good salary, she wasn't able to build the wealth she had hoped for. She kept her savings in low-interest accounts, worried about losing any of it.

Sophie, however, saw her wealth grow steadily. She wasn't just saving; she was building assets. Over time, her investments in the stock market and real estate appreciated. She also worked on building a side business that provided passive income. Because of her belief in abundance; her belief that money could grow with the right strategies, Sophie was able to make decisions that set her up for long-term financial freedom. When she faced financial challenges, she didn't panic. She adapted, learned, and adjusted her approach. Sophie understood that the road to financial freedom wasn't linear, but with the right mindset, setbacks were just opportunities to learn and improve.

One afternoon, when the two sisters met for coffee, Lily couldn't help but admire Sophie's calm confidence. Sophie had just purchased a vacation home with the profits from her side business and was planning her next investment. Lily, meanwhile, had been feeling stuck. Despite her hard work and steady job, she had little to show for it. Her savings were enough for a rainy day, but she felt trapped by her anxieties around money.

"I don't understand, Sophie," Lily said, stirring her coffee absentmindedly. "You've always been in the same boat as me and why does it seem like you're doing so much better?"

Sophie paused, studying her sister with gentle understanding. "I think it's because of how we see money, Lily," she said softly. "You see it as something scarce, something that's always slipping away from you. I see it as something I can manage and grow."

Lily frowned. "But I work so hard. Why isn't it enough?"

Sophie smiled. "It's not just about hard work, Lil. It's about how you think about money. If you believe there will never be enough, you'll always feel anxious, no matter how much you earn. But if you believe that money is a tool that can be used, managed, and invested wisely, it changes everything. Your mindset shapes your actions and your actions shape your results."

Lily looked down at her cup, the weight of Sophie's words sinking in. "But what if I fail? What if I take risks and it all falls apart?"

"That's the scarcity mindset talking," Sophie replied gently. "It's normal to be afraid of risk, but you have to reframe it. Think of failure as a lesson, not a disaster. You can learn, adjust, and keep going."

Sophie shared with Lily the mindset shifts she had made over the years: learning to embrace opportunities, taking calculated risks, and seeing money as a vehicle for growth, not a finite resource to hoard.

Moral of the story

The story of Lily and Sophie illustrates that financial success is not solely determined by circumstances but by mindset and actions. A scarcity mindset, like Lily's, breeds fear and stagnation, while an abundance mindset, like Sophie's, fosters growth, adaptability, and empowerment. The moral is clear: **your beliefs about money shape your financial reality.**

By viewing money as a tool rather than a limitation, and by embracing learning, calculated risks, and resilience, anyone can shift from surviving to thriving. Success isn't about how much you earn but how you think, manage, and grow what you have.

Chapter 3
Building Wealth Through Habits

The importance of consistency in achieving financial goals

Success in finance is not about making one big win; it's about building habits that compound over time. This chapter focuses on creating daily financial habits that can lead to long-term wealth.

Small, consistent actions are the building blocks of wealth. Whether it's saving a small percentage of income, avoiding impulse purchases, or investing regularly, the habits you form today will create your financial reality tomorrow.

Financial habits operate like any other habit loop. Identifying the triggers that lead to poor financial decisions and replacing them with better routines can help break the cycle of debt, overspending, or lack of savings.

Setting up automatic savings, bill payments, and investments can eliminate friction and ensure that you consistently contribute toward your financial goals. Automation is one of the easiest ways to form sustainable habits and remove decision fatigue.

Celebrating even small victories, such as reaching a savings milestone or paying off a credit card, can reinforce good habits and keep you motivated. Regularly tracking your financial progress ensures you stay on course and can make adjustments if needed.

What if I told you that the key to wealth is not found in one grand decision, but in the small, consistent habits we practice every day?

Building wealth isn't about getting lucky, winning the lottery, or inheriting a fortune. It's about taking control of your financial life through the habits you form, the decisions you make, and the mindset you cultivate. So let's dive into how we can build wealth one habit at a time.

Why habits matter?

Think about it: Every action you take today, whether big or small, shapes your future. Wealth doesn't come overnight. It's a result of the choices we make consistently over time. That's where habits come in. Wealth-building habits are those little, seemingly insignificant things you do daily that add up over the long term.

In fact, habits are often more important than willpower or motivation. While motivation might get you started, it's your habits that will keep you moving toward your financial goals.

Habits are the building blocks of long-term success, particularly in the realm of personal finance. Every action you take today, no matter how small, contributes to shaping your future. Financial wealth and stability don't appear overnight, they are the cumulative result of consistent, intentional actions over time. This is the essence of why habits matter: they transform fleeting intentions into sustained progress, bridging the gap between dreams and reality.

Key habits to build wealth

Saving consistently

1. Establishing financial security:
   Consistent saving provides a safety net

for unexpected expenses. Whether it's a medical emergency, a car repair, or sudden job loss, having a reserve of savings prevents you from relying on high-interest credit cards or loans.

- A habit of saving ensures that financial emergencies are manageable, reducing stress and providing peace of mind.

2. The power of compounding:
Saving regularly, even in small amounts, allows you to benefit from compound interest. Over time, your savings grow exponentially as interest earns interest. This effect is magnified the earlier you start and the more consistently you contribute to your savings.

- For example, saving $100 monthly at an annual interest rate of 5% can grow to over $15,000 in 10 years, and more than $40,000 in 20 years.

3. Creating opportunities for wealth building:
Saving consistently is the first step toward investing. By building a habit of setting aside money, you create the capital needed to grow your wealth through investments such as stocks, mutual funds, or real estate.

- Saving acts as the gateway to financial growth, enabling you to take calculated risks that yield higher returns over time.

The Importance of prioritizing savings

- Paying yourself first:
The principle of "paying yourself first" means treating savings as a non-negotiable expense, just like rent or utilities.

By allocating money to savings before spending on discretionary items, you ensure that your financial future takes precedence over short-term desires.

- This practice instills discipline, prevents overspending, and guarantees that you're consistently setting aside money for your goals.

• Overcoming common excuses:
Many people delay saving, thinking they'll start once they earn more. However, this mindset often leads to missed opportunities. The key is to save consistently, even if the amount is small.

- Saving $20 a week may seem insignificant, but over a year, that's over $1,000, enough to kickstart an emergency fund or an investment account.

Budgeting and Tracking Expenses
Many people struggle with their finances not because they don't earn enough, but because they don't know where their money is going. Without visibility into your spending habits, it's easy to lose track of how small, seemingly harmless expenses add up over time.

- For example, daily coffee shop purchases or unused subscription services can siphon away significant amounts of money without you realizing it.

Budgeting and expense tracking allow you to align your spending with your financial goals. By understanding where your money is going, you can prioritize what matters most—whether it's saving for a home, reducing debt, or investing for the future.

Here I want to give you some practical steps for Budgeting and Expense Tracking

1. Choose a Budgeting Method:

   - 50/30/20 Rule: Allocate 50% of your income to needs, 30% to wants, and 20% to savings or debt repayment.

   - Zero-based budgeting: Assign every dollar a purpose, ensuring that income minus expenses equals zero.

   - Envelope system: Use cash envelopes for discretionary spending categories like groceries and entertainment.

2. Review and adjust monthly:
   Analyze your spending at the end of each month. Identify areas where you overspent and opportunities to cut back or reallocate funds. Adjust your budget accordingly for the next month.

3. Automate where possible:
   Automate savings and recurring payments to reduce the mental load of managing your finances. This ensures you prioritize saving and bill payments before discretionary spending.

Investing wisely

While saving is a critical first step in achieving financial security, saving alone has limitations. Savings accounts typically offer low returns, and inflation erodes the purchasing power of money over time. To build significant wealth, you must move beyond saving and embrace investing. Investing allows your money to grow exponentially by leveraging the power of compound interest and market growth, making it an indispensable part of wealth-building.

Why, dear reader of this book, saving alone isn't enough?

Low returns
Traditional savings accounts often offer minimal interest rates, barely keeping pace with inflation. This means that while your savings might grow slightly in nominal terms, their real value (purchasing power) may stagnate or even decrease over time.

1. For example, an account with a 1% annual interest rate won't compete with an inflation rate of 3%, leading to a net loss in value.

Missed growth opportunities
Money in a savings account remains static, whereas invested money has the potential to generate significant returns through market growth. Investing allows you to put your money

to work, creating opportunities for passive income and long-term wealth accumulation.

- Compound interest:
  Compound interest is one of the most powerful forces in finance. It allows your investments to grow not only on the principal amount but also on the returns generated over time. The earlier you start investing, the more you benefit from this exponential growth.

  - For instance, investing $10,000 at a 7% annual return will grow to nearly $20,000 in 10 years and over $76,000 in 30 years, even without additional contributions.

- Beating inflation:
  Investing provides returns that outpace inflation, preserving and increasing the real value of your money. Assets like stocks, real estate, and mutual funds

typically offer higher long-term returns compared to the inflation rate, ensuring your wealth grows in real terms.

- Diversified growth opportunities: Investing offers a range of asset classes, stocks, bonds, mutual funds, real estate, and more, each with unique risk and return profiles. Diversification reduces risk while capitalizing on growth opportunities across different sectors and markets.

Living below your means

Living below your means is one of the most effective and sustainable habits for building wealth. It involves spending less than you earn, regardless of your income level, and channeling the surplus into savings and investments. While it may sound simple, this habit requires discipline and a long-term perspective, especially as lifestyle inflation, the tendency to spend more as income grows, becomes a common challenge. Mastering the art of living below your means unlocks financial freedom, stability, and the ability to grow wealth over time.

Why living below your means matters?

- Creating a surplus for savings and investments:
  Spending less than you earn ensures there is money left over at the end of each month. This surplus can be directed toward an emergency fund, savings, or investments that build long-term wealth.

    - Example: If your income increases by $500 a month and you resist upgrading your lifestyle, you can save or invest the entire amount. Over time, this surplus can grow substantially through compounding.

- Avoiding debt and financial stress: Overspending often leads to reliance on credit cards, loans, and other forms of debt to maintain a lifestyle. Living below your means eliminates this risk, helping you avoid the financial stress that comes with high-interest debt.

    - By keeping expenses modest, you reduce the likelihood of falling into a debt trap and ensure that your money works for you, not against you.

- Building financial resilience: A modest lifestyle provides flexibility to handle unexpected expenses or economic downturns without compromising your financial security. Living below your means creates a financial cushion that allows you to adapt to life's uncertainties.

- Fostering long-term wealth-building: The money saved by living below your means can be invested, generating returns that contribute to financial independence. By keeping expenses steady while income grows, you accelerate the process of wealth accumulation.

The challenge of lifestyle inflation

What is lifestyle inflation?
Lifestyle inflation occurs when increased income leads to higher spending, often on non-essential upgrades such as luxury items, dining out, or a larger home. This habit prevents many individuals from building wealth, as higher earnings are matched, or exceeded, by higher expenses.

How to resist lifestyle inflation:

1. Set clear financial goals: Having specific objectives, such as saving for retirement, paying off debt, or investing in real estate, helps prioritize long-term benefits over short-term indulgences.

2. Celebrate modestly: Reward yourself in meaningful but budget-friendly ways when income grows, rather than making significant lifestyle upgrades.

Continuous learning and self-improvement

Continuous learning and self-improvement are essential for financial success. In a rapidly changing world, where financial markets, investment opportunities, and economic conditions evolve constantly, staying informed and adaptable is critical. By dedicating time to expanding your knowledge of personal finance, investing, and wealth-building strategies, you equip yourself with the tools to make informed decisions, avoid costly mistakes, and seize opportunities that others might overlook.

Knowledge is power
Understanding the principles of personal finance empowers you to take control of your financial future. Many financial mistakes, like overspending, taking on unnecessary debt, or missing out on investment opportunities, stem from a lack of knowledge.

- For example, learning about compound interest can inspire early investment, while understanding debt management strategies can help you avoid financial pitfalls.

Adapting to a changing financial landscape
The financial world is dynamic, with new technologies, investment options, and economic trends emerging regularly. Staying informed al-

lows you to adapt your strategies to current realities.

- For instance, understanding cryptocurrency or ESG (environmental, social, governance) investing could open doors to modern opportunities that align with your goals.

Making informed decisions

The more you learn, the better equipped you are to evaluate financial options critically. Whether it's selecting the right investment portfolio, negotiating a salary, or choosing between a fixed-rate and variable-rate mortgage, knowledge gives you the confidence to make decisions aligned with your goals.

Building confidence and reducing fear

Fear of the unknown often prevents people from taking action, especially in areas like investing or entrepreneurship. Education demystifies complex financial concepts, replacing uncertainty with confidence.

Avoiding Bad Debt

Debt, when used strategically, can be a powerful tool to build wealth. However, not all debt is created equal. While certain types of debt, such as a mortgage or student loan, can contribute to long-term financial growth, bad debt—such as high-interest consumer debt—can quickly erode your financial stability and derail wealth-building efforts. Learning to distinguish between good and bad debt and cultivating the habit of avoiding bad debt is essential for achieving financial independence and long-term security.

Understanding Good Debt vs. Bad Debt

Good Debt:

Definition: Debt that is used to acquire appreciating assets or increase earning potential.

Examples: Mortgages, student loans, or business loans.

Benefits:

- A mortgage helps you buy property, which typically appreciates in value over time.

- A student loan enables you to invest in education, increasing future earning potential.

- Business loans can finance ventures that generate income or build wealth.

- Good debt often comes with lower interest rates and contributes to financial growth when managed responsibly.

Bad Debt:

Definition: Debt incurred to purchase depreciating assets or for consumption without long-term benefits.

Examples: Credit card debt, payday loans, and financing for luxury items or unnecessary expenses.

1. Risks:

    - High interest rates make it difficult to pay off, leading to a cycle of borrowing and escalating debt.

    - It does not contribute to asset building or increased earning potential.

2. Bad debt drains resources, reduces savings potential, and limits financial flexibility.

Why Avoiding Bad Debt is Crucial?

High-Interest Costs:
Bad debt, such as credit card debt, often comes with exorbitant interest rates—ranging from 15% to 30% annually. These rates can cause balances to grow exponentially, making repayment increasingly difficult.

- Example: A $5,000 credit card balance at a 20% annual interest rate can take years to pay off, costing thousands in interest.

- Reduced wealth-building capacity: Money spent on interest payments could otherwise be used for savings, investments, or paying off good debt. Bad debt robs you of opportunities to grow wealth and achieve financial goals.

- Financial stress and instability: Carrying bad debt can lead to chronic financial stress, as payments consume a significant portion of your income. This instability limits your ability to plan for the future or handle emergencies.

- Impact on credit score:
High credit card balances or missed payments can damage your credit score, making it harder to secure favorable terms for good debt, such as mortgages or car loans.

The Power of Consistency

The key to all of these habits is consistency. Just like working out or eating healthy, the results of these habits might not be immediate, but they build over time. The more you stick to your financial habits, the more wealth you'll accumulate without even thinking about it.

Wealth-building is like planting a tree. At first, it's just a tiny sapling, but with patience and care, it grows strong and produces fruit. The same goes for your finances; every small action you take today will compound and grow into something much larger in the future.

Finally, let's talk about the mindset that underpins all of these habits. Building wealth isn't just about numbers, it's about adopting the right mindset. You need to believe that you can improve your financial situation through consistent effort. You need to focus on long-term goals, not short-term rewards. And you need to have the patience to see the results of your efforts.

Developing a mindset of abundance, where you see opportunities to grow, rather than focusing on limitations, will also help you cultivate the habits that lead to financial success.

Building wealth isn't about a single large decision or a lucky break. It's about the everyday choices we make, the habits we form, and the mindset we cultivate. If you want to build wealth, start small, stay consistent, and let your habits do the heavy lifting. It won't always be easy, but with the right habits, you'll set yourself up for long-term financial success.

So, let's take charge of our financial future. Start today by building the habits that will create the wealth you want tomorrow.

The Story of Elena

Once upon a time, in a bustling city filled with endless opportunities, there lived a young woman named Elena. Elena was smart, ambitious, and had big dreams of owning her own home, traveling the world, and retiring early to spend more time with her family. She worked hard as a graphic designer, but like many people, she struggled with managing her money. Despite earning a decent salary, Elena found it difficult to save for her future. She would often splurge on things she didn't need, like new clothes, gadgets, and spontaneous trips.

Elena's financial situation was comfortable, but she knew it could be better. She could never seem to stick to a budget, and whenever she tried to save for a goal, life's unexpected expenses seemed to get in the way. She had been dreaming of buying a home for years, but every time she tried to save for a down payment, something came up like a car repair, an emergency, or an unplanned vacation. The dream seemed so far out of reach.

One day, Elena attended a personal finance seminar hosted by a local bank. The speaker, an experienced financial planner named Tom, began the seminar with a simple but profound statement:

"It's not how much you make, but how consistently you save that leads to financial success."

At first, Elena didn't fully grasp what Tom meant. After all, she thought, "I make good money. Why can't I save enough?"

But as the seminar continued, Tom shared an example that clicked for Elena. He told the story of two people: Anna and Ben.

Anna and Ben: A tale of two saving strategies

Tom explained that Anna and Ben were both in their early 30s, both made a similar income, and both had similar goals which it was to save for a down payment on a home. However, they approached saving in very different ways.

Anna's approach: Anna had a big goal; she wanted to save $30,000 for a home in two years. So, at the start of the year, she decided to save $1,250 per month. At first, she was really committed. She cut out all unnecessary expenses, stopped eating out, and avoided shopping for new clothes. However, about three months into her saving plan, Anna's life started to get busy. A close friend had a wedding she couldn't miss, and her car broke down unexpectedly. To cover the expenses, Anna used some of her savings. She kept trying to catch up, but the pressure mounted, and by the end of the year, Anna had only saved $8,000, far short of her goal.

Ben's approach: Ben, on the other hand, didn't try to save a huge amount all at once. Instead, he made a smaller, more consistent plan. He decided to save just $500 a month. While he didn't sacrifice everything, he prioritized saving first. He set up an automatic transfer from his paycheck into a separate savings account so that he didn't even have to think about it. Ben's savings were small, but he stuck to his plan. When life threw him curveballs such as a surprise medical bill, a spontaneous trip with friends, he didn't dip into his savings. He simply continued saving his $500 every month, no matter what.

At the end of two years, Ben had saved $12,000, which was not enough for a home, but it was a solid foundation. The key was that he was consistent, month in and month out. And the best part? His habit of saving $500 a month was automatic. Even if Ben faced setbacks, he didn't stop. Over time, his savings grew, and as his income increased, so did his monthly savings.

The Lesson: Consistency over perfection

Elena was struck by the difference in these two approaches. Anna had tried to save aggressively, but when life got in the way, her savings were derailed. On the other hand, Ben took a slower, more methodical approach, but he stuck to it, building a strong habit of saving.

Tom explained to the seminar attendees, "In personal finance, consistency is far more important than perfection. It's not about making huge sacrifices or saving large sums of money all at once. It's about developing habits that you can maintain over time."

Consistency, Tom explained, compounds. The more you do something regularly, the easier it becomes. The small monthly savings that Ben made—while modest—added up over time. Elena realized that it wasn't the size of her savings that mattered most, but the habit of saving and the discipline to make it automatic.

Inspired by Ben's strategy, Elena decided to take action. She couldn't save $1,250 a month, but she could afford $300 per month to start. So, she set up an automatic transfer to her savings account every pay check. It wasn't much, but it was consistent. She didn't change her lifestyle drastically and she didn't stop having fun or stop spending money on things that made her happy. But she made sure to prioritize her future by setting that money aside first.

Over the next six months, Elena didn't notice the immediate results, but her balance began to grow. She celebrated small milestones like her first $1,000 saved, then $2,000, and so on. Gradually, Elena started looking for small ways to cut back on unnecessary spending, not because she had to, but because she wanted to accelerate her goal.

As the years went by, Elena's financial situation changed. She got a raise at work, which meant she could save more each month. She still kept the same habit, making it automatic. By the time Elena reached her goal of $30,000, it didn't feel like a huge stretch anymore. She had the discipline, the habit, and the mindset to reach it.

Even though it took longer than she originally planned, Elena achieved her goal, and along the way, she learned an invaluable lesson: consistency wasn't just the key to her financial success; it was the key to success in all areas of life.

The moral of the story

Elena's story teaches us that consistency is the real secret to achieving financial goals. It's easy to get discouraged when you don't see immediate results, but when you stick to a plan and make saving a habit, even small amounts can add up over time. Whether you're saving for retirement, a home, or an emergency fund, the key is regular, consistent action.

Just like Ben in the story, who saved $500 a month even when life threw curveballs, you too can build wealth over time by being patient, setting realistic goals, and staying consistent. Remember, slow and steady wins the race!

Chapter 4
Overcoming Financial Setbacks and Staying Motivated

Everyone faces setbacks on their financial journey, whether it's a job loss, unexpected expenses, or market downturns. This chapter provides strategies for overcoming challenges and staying motivated when things aren't going as planned.

Fear of loss, fear of failure, and fear of making mistakes can be paralysing. By acknowledging these fears and reframing them, you can take proactive steps to protect your financial well-being while moving toward your goals.

Every setback offers valuable lessons. Whether you made a poor investment choice, overspent on a luxury, or faced a job loss, these challenges can be used as stepping stones to future success. Reflect, learn, and adjust.

Surrounding yourself with like-minded individuals who share your financial goals can be incredibly motivating. Whether it's through a support group, mentor, or accountability partner, having others to share successes and challenges with can keep you focused and motivated.

Whether it's an unexpected medical bill, job loss, a failed investment, or simply living through difficult times, financial setbacks can feel overwhelming. But here's the truth: setbacks don't define us. How we respond to them is what truly shapes our financial future.

Understanding financial setbacks

First, let's acknowledge what a financial setback is. It's anything that disrupts your financial stability or progress. It could be a loss of income, an unexpected expense, or even a mistake you made with money. These moments can cause stress, self-doubt, and sometimes even fear about the future. But remember: setbacks **are a natural part of life**. They happen to everyone, and they are not the end of the story.

The key is how we choose to react when these challenges arise.

The Power of resilience

One of the most important qualities in overcoming financial setbacks is resilience; the ability to bounce back. Resilience isn't something we're born with; it's a skill we can develop over time. In fact, some of the most successful people have faced significant setbacks, yet they found ways to persevere and emerge stronger. They didn't let their situation define them; they took control and worked toward a better future.

Steps to overcome financial setbacks

So, how do we overcome these financial challenges? Here are a few key steps to help you navigate through tough times:

1. Acknowledge the setback, but don't dwell on it

The first step is to acknowledge the setback. It's important to accept that financial difficulties are part of life. Denying the reality of the situation will only keep you stuck. However, once you acknowledge the setback, don't dwell on it. Negative emotions like regret, guilt, or frustration may arise, but it's crucial not to let them hold you back. Instead of focusing on what went wrong, focus on what you can do to move forward.

2. Take a step back and assess the situation

When faced with a financial setback, it's easy to get overwhelmed. But when emotions calm down, take a step back and assess the situation logically. Write down the problem, identify its cause, and determine how serious it is. Is it a temporary cash flow issue, or is it a deeper financial problem? This will help you break down the situation and create a plan to address it.

3. Create a recovery plan

Once you have a clear understanding of the problem, create a plan to get back on track. This could involve cutting back on spending, finding additional sources of income, or revisiting your budget. If your setback is debt-related, consider speaking to a financial advisor or exploring debt repayment options like consolidation or refinancing.

4. Focus on what you can control

Financial setbacks often make us feel powerless, but the key is to focus on what you can control. You may not be able to change the past, but you can take action in the present. This could mean adjusting your spending habits, learning about financial planning, or setting up an emergency fund to avoid future setbacks.

5. Seek support and professional advice

Remember, you don't have to go through this alone. Seek support from family, friends, or a financial advisor. Sometimes, talking through a problem with someone else helps you see things from a different perspective. A professional can also provide practical advice on how to recover from financial challenges, whether it's managing debt, improving your credit score, or rebuilding your savings.

6. Learn from the setback

Every setback holds a lesson. Whether you've learned something about your spending habits, your investment strategies, or your financial priorities, take the opportunity to learn and grow. View your setback as a lesson rather than a failure. This mindset shift will not only help you recover faster but also make you more financially resilient in the future.

Financial setbacks don't have to derail your progress—they can be stepping stones on the path to financial resilience. By building strong financial habits, such as budgeting, saving, and investing consistently, you create a financial foundation that can withstand the unexpected. An emergency fund, for example, can act as a buffer in tough times, allowing you to handle setbacks with more ease and confidence.

The Story of Marcus

Marcus had always prided himself on his ability to make good decisions. He had a steady job as a sales manager at a tech company, and in his early 30s, he was already starting to feel like he had a handle on life. He was living comfortably, making enough to cover his bills, put some money aside, and enjoy the occasional splurge. He had even started saving for his dream of owning a house.

But everything changed one rainy Tuesday morning when Marcus received an email that would alter the course of his life.

The Setback: Losing his job

The email was from his boss. Due to unforeseen budget cuts, Marcus's entire department was being laid off. "Due to the economic downturn, we regret to inform you that your position has been eliminated effective immediately."

The shock was instantaneous. His heart raced. How could this happen? He had always been a top performer at work, but now, Marcus found himself facing an uncertain future. With no job lined up and no backup plan, his immediate concern was money.

Marcus had always considered himself financially responsible, but he quickly realized he had no real emergency fund and he pretty much had just a few months of living expenses. He had been focused on other things such as buying a car, going on vacations, and treating himself. Does it sounds familiar to you?

I believe if you are reading this book is because you found yourself exactly in the same position, but let's get back to Marcus.

He had never prepared for a situation like this, where his income could suddenly disappear.

As the days turned into weeks, Marcus sent out dozens of resumes, but the job market was tough. He began to dip into his savings, but it didn't take long for him to feel the stress of watching his bank balance shrink. His dream of homeownership seemed to slip further away. Every small purchase now felt like a luxury.

The Despair: Facing financial pressure

Three months later, things had not improved. Marcus had taken a few temp jobs here and there, but nothing had stuck. The strain on his finances was starting to affect his mental health. He had to scale back on everything—no more eating out, no new clothes, no weekend trips. He sold his car to downsize to something more affordable. But despite his best efforts, the bills continued to pile up, and his savings dwindled.

One evening, after a particularly frustrating day of job hunting, Marcus sat in his small apartment, staring at his credit card bills, wondering how he was going to make it through another month. He felt defeated.

But just as he was about to give in to despair, his phone rang. It was his older brother, Derrick, who had always been his source of support during tough times.

"How's it going, man?" Derrick asked, sounding upbeat as usual.

Marcus let out a deep sigh. "Not great. I've been struggling to find something permanent, and my savings are almost gone. I'm not sure how much longer I can keep this up."

Derrick paused for a moment, then said something that would stick with Marcus for a long time.

"You know, Marcus, I've been through my own financial struggles in the past. Losing my job a few years ago was one of the hardest things I ever went through. But here's what I learned: it's not about avoiding challenges. It's about building the resilience to bounce back when things don't go as planned. You have the strength to turn this around. You just need to change your mindset."

A new mindset

At first, Marcus didn't know what Derrick meant by "resilience." But as he thought about it, he began to realize that his focus had always been on avoiding failure or setbacks. He had been so preoccupied with being in control and having everything go according to plan that he never anticipated the inevitable bumps along the way. And when those bumps hit, he felt like he was falling apart.

But Derrick's words made him rethink his approach. Resilience wasn't about avoiding hardship—it was about how you recover from it. Marcus realized that he had been letting his circumstances define his future instead of taking control of his situation.

The next day, Marcus made a decision. He would stop viewing his financial struggles as a setback he couldn't overcome. Instead, he would treat this period as an opportunity to build resilience and to learn new skills, rethink his priorities, and set himself up for future success. It wouldn't be easy, but he would adapt and bounce back.

Taking action

With his new mindset in place, Marcus took several steps to rebuild his financial life.

1. Creating a strict budget

The first thing he did was sit down and create a strict budget. He cut out all unnecessary expenses. No more ordering takeout, no more entertainment subscriptions, and no more shopping for things he didn't need. He focused on essentials: food, utilities, and small amounts for mental health, like a weekly walk in the park or reading books to keep his mind active.

2. Rebuilding his emergency fund

Marcus also made it a priority to rebuild his emergency fund. He knew that having financial security in the form of 3-6 months' worth of living expenses was a must moving forward. Even though he was still unemployed, he set aside a portion of his remaining savings each month. It wasn't much, but it gave him a sense of security knowing that he had a buffer to fall back on.

3. Networking and learning new skills

Marcus knew that relying solely on job applications wasn't going to be enough. He turned to his network of friends, former colleagues, and even people in industry-specific online groups. He attended virtual career fairs and connected with people who had navigated the same challenges. In the process, he realized that some of his skills were outdated. So, Marcus enrolled in a few free online courses to enhance his expertise in digital marketing, something he could apply to his next job.

4. Taking small, steady steps toward stability

He also decided to take on temporary work whenever he could, doing freelance marketing projects or offering digital services on the side. These small steps didn't bring in huge amounts of money, but they helped him build back his confidence, stay productive, and meet some of his expenses.

The Comeback: Turning the corner

Six months after losing his job, Marcus had made significant strides. He had rebuilt his emergency fund, developed new skills, and started networking more actively. His financial situation had improved slightly, though he was still working on getting back to where he wanted to be.

But the real breakthrough came when he landed an interview at a growing startup. His freelance experience and his recent skills training helped him stand out. When he got the call offering him the job, Marcus felt an overwhelming sense of relief and pride.

But it wasn't just about the job. It was about the journey he had gone through and the resilience he had built in the face of adversity. Marcus realized that bouncing back wasn't just about having the right resources. It was about having the right mindset. His ability to adapt, learn, and keep pushing forward was what had allowed him to recover, both financially and mentally.

The Lesson: Building resilience for financial success

Marcus's story teaches us a critical lesson: resilience is not just about surviving financial setbacks; it's about learning from them and using them as a foundation for future success. When life throws you a curveball, whether it's losing a job, dealing with unexpected expenses, or facing a financial crisis....well amigo, the key is *not to give up*, but to adapt, learn, and grow stronger.

Taking control of what you can control—your actions, your mindset, and your habits.

Learning from challenges instead of letting them defeat you.

Staying flexible and adjusting your financial goals when life changes.

Building an emergency fund and other safety nets so that when the unexpected happens, you're prepared to face it.

In the end, it wasn't the challenges that defined Marcus but it was his ability to bounce back and keep moving forward. And that resilience would serve him far beyond his financial struggles as it would help him thrive, no matter what life threw his way.

The story of Maya.

Maya had always prided herself on her financial independence. She had spent years building a career as a graphic designer, steadily growing her savings, and building a small portfolio of investments. Her friends would often admire how she seemed to have it all together like working hard, living frugally, and setting long-term goals. For a while, everything felt under control.

But then, in the span of a few months, everything changed.

A major client who accounted for half of Maya's income suddenly cancelled their contract, leaving her scrambling to find new work. To make matters worse, just as her income started to dwindle, her car broke down, and a significant medical expense popped up, all at once. Her savings, which had once felt like a cushion of security, started to deplete quickly.

It felt like she was drowning in a sea of bills, deadlines, and worries. Her credit card balances began to rise, and the anxiety about not having enough money started to seep into every aspect of her life.

One evening, as she sat staring at her bank account, feeling the weight of her situation pressing down on her, Maya asked herself: How did this happen?

It wasn't just the money but it was the emotional toll that came with it. Maya had always prided herself on her financial discipline, but now she felt like a failure. She felt like everything she had worked for was slipping through her fingers.

The fear of not being able to recover, of losing the financial freedom she had worked so hard to build, was overwhelming.

The Struggle

For the next few weeks, Maya tried everything to get back on track. She cut back on everything and cancelled subscriptions, stopped going out with friends, and even sold a few things from her apartment. Despite her best efforts, the financial pressure never seemed to ease. Each time she managed to pay down a little bit of debt, another unexpected expense would come up.

Her confidence began to waver. She was used to being self-reliant, but now she found herself constantly questioning her decisions. "Maybe I wasn't cut out for this freelance life," she thought. "Maybe I should have taken that full-time job offer when I had the chance."

There were moments when Maya felt like giving up and closing her business and finding a stable job, or simply pretending the problem didn't exist. She wanted to hide from the stress, to stop worrying, to find a quick fix. But deep down, she knew that this was a turning point. She couldn't afford to give up, for sure not now.

One day, while scrolling through social media, Maya stumbled upon a post from an old friend named Ethan. Ethan had always been the type of person to bounce back quickly from setbacks. His post was about his own financial journey: he had gone through a period of serious debt after a failed business venture but had turned things around by focusing on building resilience.

Ethan's words struck a chord with her: "It's not about how fast you bounce back, it's about how you build the strength to keep going. Resilience is the key."

Maya realized that she needed to stop focusing on the crisis and start focusing on what she could control: her mindset. She had been reactive, overwhelmed by circumstances, but now it was time to take action and rebuild with intention.

The decision to build resilience

Maya decided it was time to face her financial challenges head-on. Instead of ignoring the problem or waiting for a miracle, she needed to embrace the process of recovery.

She started by reframing her situation. Rather than seeing herself as a victim of her circumstances, Maya began to think of herself as a resilient person, someone who had the ability to adapt and rise above adversity.

The first step was to create a clear plan. Maya began by assessing her expenses, setting aside time each week to review her financial situation. She reached out to a few clients she had worked with in the past and started looking for new projects. Slowly but surely, she began to rebuild her income.

But it wasn't just about finding new work. Maya realized that resilience didn't just come from bouncing back quickly and it came from learning and growing from the experience. She took a hard look at her past financial habits and identified areas for improvement:

- Building a stronger emergency fund: Maya committed to building a larger cushion this time, something that would truly cover her for a few months if needed.

- Smart budgeting: She set up a more structured budget, cutting unnecessary expenses while still allowing for the occasional treat to keep her motivated.

- Reinvesting in herself: Maya enrolled in a financial literacy course to better understand investing and saving strategies, ensuring she was prepared for any future financial challenges.

Most importantly, Maya worked on her mindset. She made a commitment to stop viewing setbacks as failures and started to see them as learning opportunities. Every financial setback was a chance to improve her financial resilience.

The Rebuild

As the months passed, Maya's situation gradually began to improve. The combination of consistent work, a more disciplined approach to managing her money, and a growing sense of confidence allowed her to stabilize her finances. Her emergency fund grew, and her debt started to shrink.

But it wasn't just about the numbers. Maya realized that the true victory wasn't just overcoming the financial challenges, it was about learning how to handle challenges without letting them define her.

She began to build habits that would help her avoid falling into the same patterns again. When she had a quiet month, instead of panicking, she would stick to her budget and lean on her emergency fund. She developed healthier attitudes toward money, acknowledging that it was okay to face difficulties, as long as she had the resilience to get through them.

Maya also found joy in helping others who were going through similar struggles. She began offering free workshops to freelancers and small business owners in her community, sharing what she had learned about bouncing back from financial challenges. It felt empowering to not only rebuild her own financial life but to help others do the same.

The Transformation

Two years after that difficult period, Maya looked back at her financial journey and realized how far she had come—not just financially, but personally. The resilience she had developed through the hardest time in her life had transformed the way she approached challenges.

She was no longer afraid of financial setbacks. She had built the tools and strategies to bounce back, and she knew that no matter what happened, she had the strength to handle it. Most importantly, Maya understood that setbacks were part of the journey, not the end of it.

She had learned to embrace the process of growth. Every time she overcame an obstacle, she grew stronger, more confident, and more capable. The financial security she had once dreamed of was now within reach—not because of a sudden windfall or quick fix, but because she had developed the resilience to keep going, even when things felt impossible.

Maya had learned that financial success wasn't just about making money but it was about building the mental and emotional resilience to weather the storms, to adapt, and to keep moving forward.

The lesson here: Resilience is key

Maya's story is a powerful reminder that financial challenges are an inevitable part of life, but they don't define us. What defines our success is how we respond to those challenges. Building resilience means understanding that setbacks are part of the process and that we have the ability to recover and learn from them.

Resilience isn't about avoiding difficulty but it's about growing stronger in the face of adversity. By developing a resilient mindset, we can not only overcome financial challenges but thrive in the face of them. And just like Maya, we can help others along the way, creating a ripple effect of financial strength and confidence that benefits everyone.

Chapter 5
Shifting Your Mindset from Spending to Investing

This chapter focuses on shifting from a consumption-driven mindset to an investment-oriented mindset, which is crucial for long-term wealth creation.

The key to building wealth lies in acquiring **assets** (things that put money in your pocket) and avoiding **liabilities** (things that take money out of your pocket). We'll explore the differences and how to prioritize building assets.

Building wealth requires **discipline** and the ability to delay immediate gratification for future rewards. Whether it's saving money instead of spending it or investing early for long-term gains, delayed gratification is a key component of financial success.

Learning to **invest** wisely is one of the best ways to grow your wealth. I will share different investment strategies, from stock market investments to real estate and alternative investments, and how to stay motivated even when markets are volatile.

For many of us, it's easy to get caught up in the excitement of spending and buying the latest gadgets, enjoying a night out, or treating ourselves to things we want. But while spending gives us instant gratification, investing is what creates long-term wealth and financial freedom.

So, how do we make that transition? How do we shift from spending our money to investing it in ways that will benefit us in the future?

The Power of mindset

The way we think about money directly influences how we use it. If we have a mindset that prioritizes immediate pleasure or buying things we don't truly need, it's easy to fall into a cycle of consumption. But shifting to a mindset that sees money as a tool for future growth is what separates those who achieve long-term financial success from those who live pay check to pay check.

A spending mindset focuses on what can I buy right now?

An investing mindset focuses on how can I use my money to create more wealth over time?

The real key to financial success is not in how much you earn but in how much you keep and how you make that money grow.

Understanding the difference between spending and investing

First, let's break down the difference between spending and investing.

Financial success hinges on how you use your money, and a key part of that is distinguishing between spending and investing. Both are integral to life, but they serve vastly different purposes. While spending provides immediate satisfaction, investing builds long-term value and financial security. Recognizing this distinction is critical for making informed choices that balance present needs with future goals.

What is spending?

Definition:
Spending involves exchanging money for goods or services that meet immediate needs or desires but do not contribute to wealth-building.

Examples of spending:

- Buying clothes, dining out, or purchasing the latest tech gadget.

- Paying for entertainment, vacations, or convenience services like food delivery.

Purpose and value:

- Spending often enhances our quality of life, providing comfort, convenience, or enjoyment.

- While some expenditures are essential—such as housing, utilities, and groceries—many fall into the category of discretionary spending, offering short-term satisfaction without adding long-term financial value.

Impact on wealth:

- Spending money on depreciating assets (e.g., cars, electronics, or trends) or non-essential services does not grow your wealth.

- Over time, unchecked spending can deplete resources that could have been directed toward savings or investments.

What is Investing?

Definition:
Investing involves allocating money to assets or opportunities that have the potential to generate income or appreciate in value over time. It

shifts the focus from immediate gratification to long-term growth.

Examples of investing:

- Financial Assets: Stocks, bonds, mutual funds, or ETFs.

- Real Estate: Purchasing property that appreciates in value or generates rental income.

- Personal growth: Education, certifications, or starting a business to increase earning potential.

- Purpose and value:

  - Investing aims to create financial security, passive income, or wealth.

  - It prioritizes delayed gratification, with the understanding that short-term sacrifices can yield significant long-term rewards.

Impact on wealth:

- Investments grow wealth by harnessing the power of compounding, market appreciation, or income generation.

- Unlike spending, which depletes resources, investing turns money into an active contributor to your financial future.

Key differences between Spending and Investing

Aspect	Spending	Investing
Purpose	Immediate satisfaction or meeting current needs.	Building wealth or generating future income.
Time Horizon	Short-term.	Long-term.
Financial Outcome	Depletes financial resources.	Grows financial resources.
Examples	Clothes, dining out, vacations.	Stocks, real estate, education.

Why shift to an investing mindset?

Shifting from spending to investing might feel challenging at first, but the benefits are undeniable. Here's why this shift is crucial for your financial future:

Building wealth over time

When you invest, you allow your money to grow. Thanks to compound interest—the concept where the interest on your investments earns interest—you can build wealth far beyond what you could with saving alone. Over time, investments can significantly outpace the rate of inflation and create financial security.

Achieving Financial independence

A spending mindset often traps us in a cycle of working to pay for the things we think we need. An investing mindset, however, gives you the potential to earn passive income and build a financial cushion that supports your future. It can help you achieve financial independence and give you the freedom to make choices based on what you want, not just what you can afford today.

Turning money into a tool for growth

Instead of using your money solely to buy things, an investing mindset helps you see money as a tool for growth. It shifts your focus from short-term satisfaction to long-term financial security and wealth-building.

How to shift from spending to investing?

Now that we understand why shifting our mindset is important, let's talk about how to make that change.

Start with awareness

The first step is awareness. Take a close look at where your money is going. How much do you spend on things that don't contribute to your long-term goals? Are there areas where you can cut back in order to free up money for investing?

The more you understand your spending habits, the more control you can take over your financial future.

Create a budget and pay yourself first

One of the most powerful tools in shifting from spending to investing is creating a budget. This isn't about restricting yourself; it's about giving your money a purpose. A portion of your income should be automatically directed toward your investments. This "pay yourself first" strategy ensures that you prioritize investing and saving before spending on non-essential items.

Start small, but start now

You don't need a large sum of money to begin investing. Start with small amounts, even if it's just $50 or $100 per month. The key is to begin the habit of investing regularly. With time, as your confidence and income grow, so can your investments.

Focus on long-term goals

It's easy to get tempted by immediate gratification. But remember, investing is about the long game. Shift your focus from instant desires to long-term goals, such as retirement, buying a home, or building an emergency fund. Having a clear financial goal will help you stay disciplined and motivated in your investment journey.

Educate yourself

To make the most of your investments, it's essential to educate yourself. Understand the basics of investing, the types of assets you can invest in, and the risks involved. The more you know, the more confident you will be in making smart financial decisions.

Automate your investments

One of the easiest ways to stay consistent with investing is to automate it. Set up automatic transfers to a savings or investment account.

This way, you don't even have to think about it—you're investing consistently without temptation to spend the money elsewhere.

Overcoming the Fear of investing

Many people avoid investing because they fear losing money or feel overwhelmed by the complexity. But here's the truth: the earlier you start, the more time you give your money to grow, and the less impact short-term market fluctuations will have. Start by investing in low-risk options like index funds or mutual funds, and as you gain experience and confidence, you can diversify your portfolio.

The Reward of shifting your mindset

By shifting from a spending mindset to an investing mindset, you're not just making better financial decisions today you're setting yourself up for a future of financial freedom, security, and opportunities. The more you invest, the more your money works for you, rather than the other way around.

In conclusion, shifting your mindset from spending to investing is one of the most important changes you can make in your financial life. It's not always easy, but with discipline, patience, and the right knowledge, it can lead to long-term financial success. So, ask yourself today: Are you ready to start making your money work for you?

Start thinking beyond the next purchase, and start thinking about how you can invest in your future. Because when you invest in your financial growth, you're investing in your freedom.

The Story of Maria.

Maria had always been good with money. She worked as a marketing manager at a mid-sized tech company, earning a solid salary. Every month, she paid her bills, went out with friends, and treated herself to a few nice things. She lived in a comfortable apartment, drove a decent car, and had a closet full of clothes. But despite her seemingly secure financial life, Maria felt like she was always treading water.

She'd saved some money over the years, but it was mostly sitting in a checking account, earning no interest. Maria had a vague idea that investing was something rich people did, and that she wasn't "there" yet and "investing is for the people who already have money," she thought. Instead, she focused on what she could see and feel right now: the newest gadgets, vacations, dining out, and impulse purchases that brought temporary happiness.

But everything changed one night, after a conversation with her uncle, Tom, at a family gathering.

The Catalyst: A conversation with uncle Tom

Maria's uncle, Tom, had always been a quiet, unassuming man. He had never flaunted his wealth, but everyone in the family knew that he was financially well-off. He had retired early, lived comfortably, and travelled the world. He didn't have a flashy lifestyle, but he always seemed content and at ease with his financial situation.

At dinner, Tom casually mentioned that he had recently invested in some real estate and was seeing solid returns. "It's great to watch my money work for me," he said, almost offhandedly. Maria, who had always thought of investing as a mysterious, complicated world, was intrigued.

"What do you mean your money works for you?" she asked.

Tom smiled. "Well, Maria, the difference between those who get ahead financially and those who don't often comes down to one thing: mindset. When you spend, you're always chasing something external in a form of a material possessions or instant gratification. When you invest, you're putting your money to work so it can grow and build wealth for your future."

Maria was sceptical. "But isn't investing risky? And don't you need a lot of money to get started?"

Tom nodded. "There's risk in everything, but the key is to understand what you're investing in and start small. You don't need to be wealthy to invest; you just need to start with what you have and build over time. I didn't start with real estate. I started with stocks and mutual funds. But the most important shift I made was in my mindset. Instead of thinking, 'I need to spend on this,' I started thinking, 'How can I make my money work for me?'"

Maria was taken aback by Tom's simplicity. It seemed like such a small shift, yet it carried such profound weight. She realized that she had been focused on the immediate—buying the next shiny object, enjoying instant pleasure. Meanwhile, her uncle had shifted his focus to the future, thinking about how he could make his money grow, even when he wasn't working.

That night, she went home thinking about her spending habits and the long-term effects they had on her future.

The Mindset shift

The next day, Maria began reflecting on her financial habits. "What if I stopped thinking of money as something to spend, and started thinking of it as something to invest?"

At first, the idea of shifting from spending to investing felt foreign and intimidating. She had always lived enjoying her income rather than making it work for her. But the more she thought about it, the more she realized that this mindset shift could be the key to building the life she wanted with financial freedom, security, and even the ability to retire early like Uncle Tom.

Maria knew she didn't have a ton of extra cash lying around, but she did have a few key realizations:

Small changes lead to big results: She didn't have to make huge changes all at once. Even small amounts of $100 here and there could add up over time. "It's the power of compounding," she thought.

Delayed gratification: She had been spending impulsively and buying things just because she could. What if, instead, she delayed those purchases and invested that money? If she could postpone the gratification of spending today, it would lead to greater rewards in the future.

Long-term thinking: Instead of trying to keep up with trends, Maria realized she needed to focus on building long-term wealth, not short-term pleasure. "What if I invested the money I spend on designer handbags into stocks or real estate?" she asked herself.

Taking action: Starting small, thinking big

The very next month, Maria made a decision. She started by automating a portion of her paycheck into a retirement account, something she had never done before. She chose a modest amount at first, $200 per month, which didn't feel like much, but it was a start. Then, she set up a second automatic transfer to a brokerage account where she could buy individual stocks and mutual funds.

She also cut back on some of her discretionary spending and no more spontaneous shopping trips, and smaller vacations. Instead of eating out five times a week, she cooked at home more often, and redirected the money saved into her investment accounts.

Over time, Maria's perspective began to change. Investing didn't feel like a sacrifice and instead it felt like a strategy for her future. It wasn't about denying herself happiness or pleasure; it was about making sure her future self would thank her. Each time she contributed to her investment account, she felt a sense of accomplishment, knowing that she was taking care of herself long-term, not just living for the present.

She also began to educate herself more on investing. She read books, listened to podcasts, and took online courses. While investing initially seemed like a complex world, Maria began to realize that with a little education, it wasn't that hard to understand. Over time, she became more confident in her choices, making smarter investments and diversifying her portfolio.

The Reward: Seeing the fruits of her investments

After a year of investing consistently, Maria began to see results. Her retirement account was growing, and the stocks in her brokerage account had increased in value. The more she invested, the more she understood the power of compound interest and the idea that her money was growing on its own, generating returns on top of returns.

But the biggest reward was the shift in her mindset. She no longer felt like a passive participant in her financial life. Instead, she felt empowered, knowing that she was building something that would support her future.

Two years later, Maria reached her goal of having enough money to make a down payment on her first home. And the real kicker? The money she had been investing over the past two years had grown so much that her down payment was larger than she initially expected. She no longer had to depend on credit or loans to make big purchases; her investments had allowed her to live comfortably and buy her dream home—without jeopardizing her long-term financial security.

The Lesson: Shifting your mindset from spending to investing

Maria's journey shows us that the most powerful thing we can change is not our bank account balance, but our mindset. Shifting from a mindset of spending to a mindset of investing isn't just about cutting back or making sacrifices. It's about choosing long-term growth over short-term gratification. It's about making your money work for you, instead of working just to spend it.

For Maria, the change wasn't instantaneous and it took time, discipline, and education. But the key was the shift. Instead of focusing on how she could spend money, she began to think about how she could use it to build wealth. And once she made that mindset shift, everything else fell into place.

Now, when Maria thinks about her financial goals, she doesn't think about what she can buy today; she thinks about what she can invest in today that will bring her greater returns tomorrow. And that mindset, above all, has been her greatest investment.

Chapter 6
Financial Freedom and the Final Push

The ultimate goal for many is financial independence which for me it's the ability to live without relying on a pay check. This chapter will provide a blueprint for achieving financial freedom and staying motivated until the finish line.

Financial independence is the ultimate goal for many and it means having enough passive income to cover your living expenses, freeing you from the need to work for money. It's not merely about accumulating wealth but about achieving the freedom to live life on your terms, pursue passions, and contribute to causes you care about. Whether through the principles of the FIRE (Financial Independence, Retire Early) movement or other strategies, achieving financial independence requires careful planning, disciplined action, and alignment with personal values.

What is financial independence?

Definition:
Financial independence occurs when your passive income, earnings from investments, rental properties, dividends, or other sources, exceeds your monthly expenses. At this stage, work becomes optional, and financial stress diminishes significantly.

Key metrics to determine your target number:

- Annual expenses x 25 rule: A common benchmark for financial independence is saving 25 times your annual expenses, based on the 4% safe withdrawal rate from your portfolio.

- Tailored goals: Your "target number" depends on your lifestyle, desired level of comfort, and financial obligations. For example, someone living a minimalist lifestyle may require far less than someone with a high-cost lifestyle.

- Freedom beyond money:
Achieving financial independence is not just about financial security but also about the ability to spend your time in meaningful ways, whether that's pursuing hobbies, traveling, or dedicating time to philanthropy.

The FIRE movement: A path to financial independence

The FIRE movement, short for Financial Independence, Retire Early, offers a structured approach to achieving financial independence faster than traditional retirement timelines. It emphasizes aggressive saving, investing, and frugality to build wealth efficiently.

Some people ask me what is the next step after achieving "the million" or simply achieving the financial freedom. Well, to me these should be the next steps to follow and I will describe them below, but my first advise is ***Live the life you wanted and just go and enjoy it!***

Life after financial independence: A values-driven approach

Achieving financial independence is a milestone, not the destination. For many, the next step is using their wealth to create a meaningful and fulfilling life.

1. **Supporting Causes You Care About:**

    ○ Financial independence allows you to dedicate resources to philanthropy or volunteering. Whether it's supporting education, environmental initiatives, or social justice, your wealth can have a positive impact.

2. **Pursuing Passions:**

    ○ With financial security, you have the freedom to explore hobbies, creative projects, or entrepreneurial ventures that align with your interests and talents.

3. **Helping Others:**

- Many financially independent individuals find fulfillment in sharing their knowledge or resources with others, mentoring, or assisting family and friends.

4. **Living Aligned with Your Values:**

- A fulfilling financial journey is not about accumulating wealth for its own sake. It's about ensuring your financial choices reflect your priorities, whether that's traveling, simplifying your lifestyle, or making the world a better place.

Financial independence is about more than money; it's about freedom, choices, and living a life aligned with your values. By setting clear goals, adopting the principles of the FIRE movement, and staying motivated through disciplined saving and investing, you can achieve financial independence earlier than most. Once reached, the true reward lies in the ability to use your wealth to pursue passions, help others, and create a meaningful life. The journey may require sacrifices, but the fulfillment of financial independence makes it a worthy endeavor.

The Story of Alex

Alex had always dreamed of financial freedom and the kind of freedom where your money works for you, not the other way around. Growing up, he didn't come from wealth. His parents were hard-working folks, but their salaries didn't leave much room for savings or investing. But Alex was different. From a young age, he was determined that he wouldn't fall into the same trap. He knew that to get ahead, he would need to break free from the cycle of living month-to-month.

In his early 30s, Alex had already achieved a lot. He had a decent job as a product manager at a tech startup, a modest but comfortable apartment, and he was on his way to paying off the student loans that had haunted him for years. But despite his progress, something always nagged at him; he wasn't financially free yet.

He had saved up a small emergency fund and invested some money in stocks, but it never felt like enough. He was still living under the shadow of "one bad financial decision" or "one unexpected bill" throwing him off track. He wasn't yet in a position to walk away from his job, travel the world, or do what he truly loved without worrying about money. Alex had heard the stories of people who achieved financial freedom and was determined that, one day, he would get there too.

But how?

The Struggle: The long road to freedom

It wasn't that Alex wasn't doing the "right" things. He had read the books, followed the blogs, and listened to podcasts about personal finance. He knew all the rules: save at least 20% of his income, avoid lifestyle inflation, invest in low-cost index funds, and build passive income. He'd cut back on expenses and no more expensive gym memberships or weekly nights out. He had eliminated his debt and made steady progress building his investment portfolio.

But there were still moments when he felt discouraged. His pay check wasn't growing as quickly as he'd hoped, and the market was unpredictable. Some of his investments had underperformed. And while his net worth was growing steadily, it seemed like it would take years, maybe even decades, before he could finally say he was financially free.

Alex also had a big dream; he wanted to eventually retire early and start his own business in digital marketing. But with the way things were going, it felt like that dream was always just out of reach. It was one of those goals that seemed so far away that it felt impossible to achieve.

One Saturday afternoon, Alex sat at his desk, staring at his financial dashboard. He had been working hard, saving as much as he could, but the finish line still seemed distant. That's when a thought hit him: "What if I could make one final push to hit my goal and take one big decision that would accelerate everything?"

He started brainstorming. He knew he needed to increase his income, but the thought of working harder at his day job wasn't appealing. He needed something that would build wealth in the long term without draining him. That's when it clicked as he had already been dipping his toes into real estate investing, but what if he took it seriously? What if he scaled up and focused on generating passive income through property?

The final push: The leap into Real Estate

Alex wasn't new to the concept of real estate. A few years back, he'd bought a small two-bedroom condo that he rented out. The rental income was decent, but it was small-scale. He thought about his current savings and realized he could leverage low-interest loans to purchase more properties. This could be the "final push" he needed to achieve his goal of financial freedom.

He spent weeks researching real estate investment strategies. He learned about house hacking, where you buy a multi-unit property, live in one unit, and rent out the others. This strategy would allow him to live for free (or even profit) while building equity in the property. It was the perfect fit and he could scale his investment portfolio and build passive income faster.

Alex decided to take action.

He sold his condo and used the profits as a down payment for a four-unit property in a growing neighbourhood. The mortgage was higher, but the rental income from the other three units would more than cover it. Plus, after factoring in property appreciation and tax benefits, he realized this investment would not only pay for itself but also generate extra cash flow every month.

The Transformation: The power of passive income

The first few months after purchasing the property were stressful. There were repairs to be made, tenants to manage, and the constant feeling of "what if something goes wrong?" But Alex was committed to his plan. He worked with a property manager to handle the day-to-day operations, allowing him to focus on his day job while building his real estate business. Slowly but surely, things started to fall into place.

Over the next year, the rental income from his new property covered his mortgage, utilities, and maintenance costs. And the best part? It freed up more of his income to invest further. With the extra cash flow, Alex purchased a second multi-family property, and then a third. Each new property generated more passive income, creating a growing snowball effect. His goal of retiring early and achieving financial independence was becoming a reality, faster than he ever imagined.

Within two years, Alex had built a portfolio of five rental properties. His rental income covered all his living expenses and more. He wasn't just financially secure and he was now financially free. His properties generated enough cash flow to allow him to quit his job and focus full-time on his real estate business, which was growing rapidly. Alex was finally in control of his time and his money.

The moment of clarity: Financial freedom achieved

One evening, as Alex sat on the balcony of his new home, watching the sunset over the city, he thought back to where he had started. The journey had been long, filled with challenges, sacrifices, and moments of doubt. But all of those sacrifices had led him here to a place where he didn't have to worry about bills, where his money was working for him, and where he had the freedom to choose how he spent his time.

That night, he logged into his financial dashboard. His rental properties, along with the stock portfolio he had built over the years, were now generating more income than he could ever spend. He could retire tomorrow, travel the world, or pursue any project he wanted.

Alex smiled, feeling a sense of pride and satisfaction. The final push had worked. Real estate investing had been the catalyst he needed to take his financial independence to the next level, but it was the combination of planning, patience, and smart decisions that had gotten him to this point.

He wasn't just financially free; he was living life on his terms.

The Lesson: The power of a final push

Alex's story demonstrates that achieving financial freedom often requires a combination of long-term strategy, patience, and sometimes, a single bold decision. For Alex, it was his leap into real estate investing that made the difference and the final push that accelerated his journey to financial independence.

But the real lesson? Financial freedom isn't just about having a large salary or making risky decisions. It's about making smart, calculated moves, being disciplined, and always looking for ways to work smarter, not harder. When you combine a clear plan with focused action, the finish line isn't as far away as it seems.

Sometimes, all it takes is that final push, whether it's a side hustle, an investment, or a change in mindset to turn your financial goals into reality. Alex's story is proof that, with persistence and strategy, anyone can achieve financial freedom and live life on their own terms.

Chapter 7
THE POWER OF SAVINGS

Saving money? Fun? You might be thinking, ...yeah, right; but hear me out. Saving money doesn't have to be about cutting back on the things you love or giving up your favourite luxuries. In fact, the real fun of saving money comes from the feeling of empowerment, freedom, and the little victories along the way. It's about winning every time you make a smart financial decision and realizing that every dollar you save is like a mini trophy, building your future one step at a time.

Here's the fun part: Saving money isn't a boring, restrictive task. When you approach it with the right mindset, it becomes a game where you win. Imagine the thrill of outsmarting impulse buys, scoring great deals, or discovering ways to enjoy life without the guilt of overspending. Saving money can be like a treasure hunt, where the treasure is your future financial freedom.

Saving money might not initially sound exciting and it's often associated with sacrifice, restriction, and missing out on luxuries. But with the right mindset, saving money transforms from a mundane task into a rewarding and even enjoyable challenge. The real fun lies not in deprivation but in empowerment, creativity, and the sense of accomplishment that comes with every smart financial choice.

Saving money doesn't have to be a chore, it can be a fun, empowering, and deeply rewarding journey. By treating it as a game, celebrating small victories, and focusing on the freedom it brings, saving becomes less about restriction and more about opportunity. With the right mindset, every dollar saved feels like a step closer to the life you envision, turning financial discipline into a thrilling and fulfilling adventure.

Here are some ways saving money can actually be fun:

1. The challenge.

Think of saving as a personal challenge. Can you go a whole week without buying that morning coffee? How about finding five things you can cut from your budget that you never even notice? These little wins add up to big victories, and each time you meet a goal, it feels like you've just unlocked a new level in a game.

1. The satisfaction of small wins.

Have you ever skipped an impulse buy and then felt like a financial ninja? That moment when you decide not to buy something you don't need and transfer that money straight into savings? It's like giving yourself a high-five for being financially savvy.

1. The thrill of finding deals.

You don't have to give up fun things to save money; you just need to be creative. Hunting for discounts, finding unique ways to enjoy activities for less, or learning how to make things last longer feels like being a savvy detective. Saving money on something you really want is like winning a mini jackpot.

1. The future dream fund.

Saving isn't just about sacrificing today but it's about investing in the future *you* want. Whether it's a trip to Bali, early retirement, or a stress-free life, every dollar you save is a step closer to that dream. And every time you save, you're funding your future self. Now *that* is fun!

1. Saving with friends.

Share the experience with others. Try a savings challenge with your friends or family and whoever saves the most in a month wins a fun prize. Turning saving into a group effort can make it feel less like a chore and more like a social game.

So, the next time you think about saving, don't see it as a sacrifice. See it as a way to level up your life with more freedom, more choices, and more fun along the way. Saving money doesn't have to be about what you give up; it's about the excitement of what you're building for the future. Who knew that a little money in the bank could make you feel like a rockstar?

Becoming financially independent without starting a business is absolutely achievable, and it doesn't require a multi-million-dollar idea or a side hustle that takes up all your time. Here are some actionable and smart strategies to help you reach financial independence, all without having to launch your own business:

Master the Art of Saving and Budgeting

The foundation of financial independence lies in saving consistently and living below your means. Start by tracking your income and expenses to understand where your money is going.

Set a budget

Create a budget that allows you to save a significant portion of your income every month and aim for at least 20-30%.

Automate savings

Set up automatic transfers to a savings or investment account to ensure you're saving first and spending second.

The key to living below your means is not about depriving yourself, but about prioritizing what truly matters. Focus on the things that bring you joy and cut back on unnecessary expenses that don't add real value to your life.

2. Invest in Index funds and ETFs

You don't have to become a stock market expert to build wealth. Index funds and ETFs

(Exchange-Traded Funds) are great options for hands-off, long-term investing.

- Diversify your portfolio: These funds typically track a broad market index (like the S&P 500), offering automatic diversification, which minimizes risk.

- Consistent contributions: Regularly contribute to your investments and think of it as paying yourself first. Over time, the power of compound interest works in your favor, and your money grows passively.

**Tip: Even small amounts invested over time can accumulate significantly. Start early and contribute consistently. You don't need a lot of money to begin, just start with what you can afford.

3. Avoid lifestyle inflation

As your income increases (whether through raises, bonuses, or other sources), resist the temptation to increase your spending in equal measure. Lifestyle inflation is a silent wealth killer.

- Keep your living expenses stable: When you get a raise, save or invest the extra income rather than upgrading your lifestyle with bigger houses, flashier cars, or more expensive habits.

- Focus on financial goals: Direct that "extra" income towards your long-term financial goals, like building an emergency fund, paying down debt, or investing for the future.

**Tip: Consider maintaining the same standard of living that got you by when you were earning less, and put the extra money into your savings or investments.

4. Live below your means, but enjoy life

Achieving financial independence doesn't mean sacrificing fun or joy, it's about intentionally allocating your money. Find ways to enjoy life on a budget:

- Prioritize experiences over things: Often, experiences (travel, hobbies, time with loved ones) bring more long-term happiness than material possessions.

- Be strategic with spending: Buy what you need, but don't be afraid to splurge on the things that really matter to you.

**Tip: The secret is balance. Enjoy life while also being mindful of where your money goes. Saving and investing shouldn't feel like punishment, it should feel like empowerment.

5. Build an emergency fund

Before you start aggressively investing or working towards financial independence, make sure you have a solid financial cushion to fall back on.

- 3-6 months of living expenses: Ideally, have enough set aside to cover 3-6 months of living expenses in case of unexpected life events (job loss, medical issues, etc.).

- Liquidity is key: Keep this fund in a low-risk, easily accessible account, like a high-yield savings account or money market fund.

**Tip: Think of your emergency fund as your financial safety net. It's not just a "rainy day" fund; it's peace of mind for when life throws you curveballs.

6. Pay off debt (Especially high-interest debt)

Debt is one of the biggest obstacles to financial independence. Focus on eliminating high-interest debt (like credit cards) as quickly as possible.

- Use the snowball or avalanche method: Pay off small debts first (snowball method) or focus on the highest-interest debts first (avalanche method).

- Avoid taking on new high-interest debt: Once you're free from high-interest debt, avoid taking on new debt that can delay your progress toward financial independence.

**Tip: The less debt you have, the less you need to earn to maintain your lifestyle. Financial independence is harder to achieve when you're weighed down by debt.

7. Increase your financial education

You don't have to become a financial expert overnight, but learning about money management can make a huge difference in your ability to make smart financial decisions.

- Read books, listen to podcasts, and take courses on personal finance, investing, and wealth-building.

- Learn the basics of investing, tax strategies, and estate planning. Understanding these concepts will help you make better choices with your money.

**Tip: The more you learn, the more confident you'll feel about making decisions that align with your goal of financial independence. Knowledge is power!

8. Focus on passive income

While you might not want to start a full-fledged business, creating streams of passive income can be a game-changer. Think of ways to make money work for you, not just rely on your paycheck.

- Rental properties: If you can, invest in real estate that generates rental income.

- Dividend stocks: Invest in stocks that pay dividends, providing you with a regular income without having to sell your investments.

- Peer-to-peer lending: Consider lending through platforms like Lending Club or Prosper to earn interest on your savings.

**Tip: The goal is to set up income streams that require little ongoing work but generate money over time. Even small streams can add up significantly in the long run.

9. Practice patience

Financial independence isn't a get-rich-quick scheme. It's about consistency, patience, and sticking to your plan over time. Building wealth takes time, but the results will be worth it.

- Track your progress: Celebrate the small wins, and keep track of how your investments and savings grow over time.

- Stay the course: The road to financial independence can be slow at times, but as long as you're disciplined, the payoff will come.

**Tip: The key to financial independence is time. The earlier you start and the more consistently you save and invest, the sooner you'll be able to reap the benefits of your efforts.

I want to offer some good advices and a comprehensive guide for you to understand your way during your journey to create prosperity.

Comprehensive guide to types of investments and wise investing strategies

Investing is a critical component of wealth-building. By understanding the types of investments available and employing smart strategies, you can grow your wealth, create passive income streams, and secure long-term financial independence. Below, we break down key investment types, explain how to invest wisely, and explore the role of investing in achieving financial success.

Types of investments

1. Stocks

- What They Are: Represent ownership in a company, giving investors a share of the company's profits through dividends or stock appreciation.

- Benefits: High growth potential, as stock values can rise significantly over time.

- Risks: Volatility is inherent, with values fluctuating due to market conditions, company performance, or economic events.

- Who it's for: Investors willing to accept higher risk for the potential of higher returns, especially those with long-term horizons.

2. Bonds

- What they are: Fixed-income securities issued by governments or corporations that pay regular interest until maturity, at which point the principal is repaid.

- Benefits: Lower risk than stocks, providing stability in a portfolio. Often used to preserve capital or generate steady income.

- Risks: Lower returns compared to stocks; vulnerable to inflation and interest rate changes.

- Who it's for: Conservative investors or those nearing retirement who prioritize stability and income over high returns.

3. Mutual Funds and ETFs (Exchange-Traded Funds)

- What they are: Pooled investments that hold a diversified portfolio of stocks, bonds, or other assets, managed by professionals. ETFs trade like stocks on exchanges.

- Benefits: Offer diversification, reducing risk by spreading investments across multiple assets. Easy for beginners and cost-effective.

- Risks: Subject to market risks, fees, and management performance.

- Who it's for: Both beginners and experienced investors looking for simplicity and diversification.

4. Real Estate

- What it is: Investment in physical properties like residential homes, commercial spaces, or land. Income can be generated through rentals, while properties often appreciate in value.

- Benefits: Tangible asset offering a hedge against inflation and portfolio diversification.

- Risks: Requires significant upfront capital and ongoing management; market downturns can reduce property values.

- Who it's for: Investors seeking stable, long-term returns and those interested in managing properties.

5. Other Assets

- What they are: Includes commodities (e.g., gold, oil), cryptocurrencies, or alternative investments like venture capital or art.

- Benefits: Unique opportunities for high returns and portfolio diversification. Commodities hedge against inflation; cryptocurrencies offer speculative potential.

- Risks: High volatility and less predictable returns; often require specialized knowledge.

- Who it's for: Advanced investors willing to explore niche markets or accept higher risks for greater rewards.

How to invest wisely

1. Start early

- Why it matters: Time is a powerful ally due to the magic of compounding, where returns on investments generate their own returns. Starting early amplifies wealth growth over decades.

- Example: Investing $200 a month starting at age 25 at a 7% annual return can grow to over $500,000 by retirement. Waiting until age 35 cuts that amount in half.

2. Diversify your portfolio

- Why it matters: Spreading investments across asset classes mitigates risk. While one asset may underperform, others may excel, balancing the overall portfolio.

- Tip: Combine stocks for growth, bonds for stability, and alternative assets for diversification.

3. Understand risk tolerance

- Why it matters: Your comfort with risk affects your investment choices. Younger investors with time to recover from market dips can take on higher risk, while older investors often prioritize capital preservation.

- How to assess: Consider factors like age, income stability, and financial goals when evaluating risk tolerance.

4. Focus on long-term growth

- Why it matters: Successful investing requires patience. Short-term market fluctuations are inevitable, but over time, markets generally trend upward.

- Example: The S&P 500 has historically delivered average annual returns of around 7-10%, despite occasional downturns.

5. Seek professional advice if needed

- Why it matters: Navigating the complexities of investing can be overwhelming. A financial advisor can help craft a personalized strategy based on your goals, time horizon, and risk tolerance.

- Tip: Ensure the advisor is reputable and understands your unique needs.

Final Thoughts: *You don't need to be a business genius to achieve **Financial independence.***

Reaching financial independence without starting a business is not only possible but totally within reach for anyone who's willing to save, invest, and make smart financial choices. By focusing on consistent savings, smart investing, reducing debt, and creating passive income, you can build wealth steadily and comfortably over time.

The best part? You don't need to be an entrepreneur, work 80-hour weeks, or have a "hustle" mentality to achieve your goals. With the right mindset and a disciplined approach, you can enjoy a life of financial freedom and the peace of mind that comes with it.

Remember, the path may not always be easy, but the rewards of financial security and independence are worth every effort. You have the power to create the future you desire so start now, and build the financial foundation that will support your dreams.

Imagine waking up every morning without the weight of financial stress hanging over you. Imagine the ability to make decisions based on what's important to you, not out of necessity or fear of running out of money. This is the promise of financial freedom.

Financial freedom doesn't mean being rich. It doesn't mean owning a mansion or driving a sports car. Financial freedom means having control over your money and your life. It means being able to live life on your own terms. It's the ability to make choices based on what brings you joy, not what you're obligated to do to survive.

Think about it: what would your life look like if money wasn't a constraint? Financial freedom opens up possibilities. It empowers you to live fully, to pursue passions, and to contribute to causes that matter to you.

The power of financial freedom

When you're financially free, you don't have to spend your days doing work you don't love just to pay the bills. You have the power to pursue your true passions, whether that's starting a business, traveling the world, or dedicating time to creative projects. Financial freedom is the key that unlocks your potential to follow your heart and create the life you've always dreamed of.

Time freedom

The most valuable resource in life isn't money but it's time. Financial freedom gives you the luxury of choosing how you spend your time. Instead of working just to make ends meet, you can spend time with family, focus on personal growth, or volunteer for a cause close to your heart. Time freedom means you can live with intention, not obligation.

Peace of mind

There's a sense of peace that comes with knowing your financial foundation is secure. No more sleepless nights worrying about how you'll pay for the next bill or where your next paycheck is coming from. With financial freedom, you have the comfort of knowing you can weather any storm, take on new opportunities, and focus on things that truly matter.

Ability to give back

With financial freedom, you're not just free to live your own life—you're free to help others live theirs. Whether it's donating to causes, supporting your community, or providing for loved ones, financial freedom allows you to make a difference in the world. It enables you to leave a legacy, not just in the form of money, but in the impact you have on others.

How to achieve financial freedom?

Achieving financial freedom is a journey, and it starts with a simple decision: I am in control of my financial future. It won't happen overnight, but with the right mindset, discipline, and strategy, it is absolutely possible.

Building financial freedom takes time. There will be setbacks, obstacles, and moments of doubt along the way. But with persistence, consistency, and a clear vision of your goals, you will get there. Financial freedom is the result of small, smart decisions made over time, not one giant leap.

The power is in your hands

Remember, financial freedom is not just a dream; it's a choice. It's a choice to take control of your financial life and make decisions that align with your goals, values, and future. It's about being proactive, taking responsibility, and knowing that you have the power to shape your destiny.

You are capable of more than you think. You have the potential to create a life of freedom, security, and purpose. All it takes is a shift in mindset, a commitment to your financial growth, and the courage to take the first step toward your future.

I want you to remember this: financial freedom is not about a dollar amount; it's about the freedom to live life the way you want to. It's the freedom to wake up excited about the possibilities ahead, the peace of mind to know you're secure, and the power to create the life you've always imagined.

So, ask yourself today: What's the life I want to create?

And then take the steps, no matter how small, toward making that life a reality.

Your future is in your hands. Let's make it a future filled with freedom, purpose, and abundance.

I hope this book helped you out to find the answers you were looking for.

www.ingramcontent.com/pod-product-compliance
Lightning Source LLC
Chambersburg PA
CBHW020648220526
45464CB00001B/345